AOTEAROA W

NEW ZEALAND
WHITEWATER

100 GREAT KAYAKING RUNS

GRAHAM CHARLES

CRAIG
POTTON
PUBLISHING

The author's moral rights have been asserted.

Published by Craig Potton Publishing, Box 555,
Nelson, New Zealand.

First published 1996.
©text: Graham Charles, 1996.
©cartoons and maps: Steve Pearce.
©photographs: as credited.

Cover photograph: Jeff Sutherland on the Turnbull River,
South Westland (Graham Charles).

ISBN 0 908802 36 6

Printed in New Zealand by Printgroup, Wellington Ltd.
Land Information New Zealand Map Licence PL098296/2.
Crown Copyright reserved.

CONTENTS

ACKNOWLEDGEMENTS

There were many people who made this project a success. I would like to thank you all. A huge thanks is due to Sarah Moodie for proofing, reproofing, writing, criticising, complimenting, directing and coaching.

Contributing writers: Sarah Moodie, Sean Waters, Linda Wensley, Bruce Barnes, Rick McGregor, Neil McKeegan, Mike Savory, Sarah McRae, Geoff Miles, Ben Willems, Donald Calder, Jonathon Hunt, Wayne Johnson.

Contributing photographers: Richard Sage, Paul Chaplow, Gordon Beadle, Peter Speirs, John Imhoof.

For answers to all the questions: Bruce and Sally Barnes, Mick Hopkinson, Baz Simmons and Katie Pidhurny, Kate Greenaway, Donald Johnstone, Gareth Eyres, Vicki Addison, Richard Sage, Ian Logie, Rick McGregor, Mark Jones, Sarah Moodie, Grant Fraser, Doug Rankin, Hugh Canard, Gordon Raynor, Gordon Beadle, Sean Waters, James McLafferty, Mahlon Nepia, Rob Worlledge, Mike Savory, Donald Calder, Gregg Beisly, Jeff Sutherland, Grant Davidson, Dave Ritchie, Jon Sanderson, Liz Blazey, Rangitata Rafts, Andi Uhl, Naomi O'Connor, Gillian Wratt, Paul Simmons, Don Allardice, Paul Chaplow, Maree Baker, Clare Cosson, Robbie Burton, Dave Chowdhury, Pete Speirs, Rangitata Rafts.

To my mentors who continue to support and believe: Mick Hopkinson, Linda Wensley, Jo Straker, Gareth Eyres, Grant Davidson.

Maps and cartoons: Steve Pearce. Maps for research: Thanks to the Department of Survey and Land Information who kindly donated the 260 Series Maps for the project. The suggested maps in the text can be obtained at any store that stocks DOSLI maps, or try calling the Info Map Centre (04 527 7019).

Boats and equipment: Perception NZ, McEwings Mountain Sports, Fairydown.

For inspiration: Donald Johnstone who is one of the greatest kayakers in the world. Whether winning slaloms, winning downriver races, winning rodeos, running extreme whitewater, enjoying an adventure, teaching, coaching or just fixing someone's car on the side of the road, Donald has unique enthusiasm, talent and charm and has worked hard for years with only some of the recognition he deserves. Thanks for everything over the years.

Finally to Linda Wensley for putting up with my monopolising the computer, van and time for the better part of six months.

FOREWORD

Information about kayaking in New Zealand was always freely available, but the trick was finding it, along with evaluating its source.

John Mackay's summer expeditions, chronicled in *Wild Rivers* went a long way to redefine masochism, but were and still are a source of information and inspiration. Graham Egarr's guide established the existence of the huge range of rivers in this country—the bulk of his work was done in the days before plastic boats! Amazing Super 8 footage of Graham Boddy in his pram dinghy accompanied by his submersible frogman friend inspired John Howard and Marty Sinclair to make the second descent (first by kayak) of the Whitcombe. Then of course there was always Hugh Canard, our own walking Encyclopedia New Zealandica. But you had to track him down!! Hugh also got frustrated enough to put out a guide to some of our better known rivers and this has served many international visitors well.

The increase in exploratory boating in the last few years has produced numerous new, quality runs. But until now you needed to know someone who knew someone who could give the lowdown on a river that you had never heard of before. Someone who knew the names of previous descenders, how many swims and broken paddles and other assorted epics they had had. Then you had to fit yourself into a nebulous pecking order to calculate how you would fare on that river in the unlikely event that you might just be graced with the same water conditions. In the process of gleaning all this information you might meet one of the legendary characters who had run the aforesaid river. Then, if you were lucky, they might check you out and even take you on one of their trips.

Both Graham Charles and I were inspired by Lars Holbeck and Chuck Stanley's guide to Sierra whitewater. Factual, humorous and accurate, it became the bible of California kayaking. We needed a similar tome.

Graham was definitely the man to do it. I first met him on the OPC Outdoor Educators Course in 1985. I was an already aging instructor and Graham was a tall spindly youth of 19. We ran a slalom on the Whanguehu for the course members, OPC staff and a group of Wanganui paddlers who happened to be there. Few rules, no numbers, you had to learn everyone's name... lots of fun. In that event I beat Graham in the slalom for the first and last time. He took up training with a vengeance and progressed to the New Zealand Slalom Team, paddling in the United States and Europe. For a while he was the apprentice on big water runs with Peter Kettering and me on the now deceased Sargood's Weir. So I have watched his development with interest... from slalomist to triathlete to whitewater and rodeo star. In his career he has forged ahead from one of the birthplaces of University of Canterbury Canoe Club paddling, the ubiquitous Mary Street flat; through jobbing instructor to chief instructor at the Sir Edmund Hillary Outdoor Pursuits Centre of New Zealand.

Everything Graham sets out to do he does intensely. His pursuit of excellence in the outdoors—whether it be mountaineering, rock climbing, kayaking or multi-sporting—has been characterised by an intense and intelligent dedication that has left people floundering in his wake.

So it was with wry amusement I watched Graham embark on this project. No stone unturned, no river unpaddled. Armed with laptop and dictaphone Graham blitzed the country in his search for accurate, useful, up-to-date information. His zeal and dedication led him and some other innocents to boldly go where no man (or non-gender specific person) has gone before. At one point he very nearly had the dubious distinction of being the first author to sink with his laptop and dictaphone, but that's his story.

I wholeheartedly endorse this guide book. The information you will find herein is straight from the horse's mouth. Graham is an expert boater and he's telling it like it is! And it's as up-to-date as is humanly possible. Only the advent of the waterproof laptop with solar panel and satellite connection to the printer will get you more up-to-date....Graham now is looking for this waterproof laptop!!

A word of advice. This isn't California with its seasonal snowmelt runoff and guaranteed weather. This is New Zealand—one of the wettest and least populated spots on earth. So, if you're going on your first helicopter trip, pick a river at least one grade lower than you normally paddle. Sharpen up your boating, check the use-by date on your rescue gear, carry split paddles, wear good portaging shoes, buy a dry suit, start studying meteorology. Good luck and good boating. You have a superb guide book in New Zealand Whitewater - Aotearoa Wai Huka.

Mick Hopkinson
Murchison
March 7, 1996

INTRODUCTION

Welcome to *New Zealand Whitewater: 100 Great Kayaking Runs*. This book has been a dream for over a decade. It represents not only a collection of facts and figures, but an offer of respect to the sport of kayaking, its characters, its sacred natural resource, and of worship to the very heart of kayaking as an adventure medium.

My impassioned involvement with the sport has spanned 12 years, eight countries and a variety of specialist disciplines within it. Some of the best and worst moments in my life have occurred participating in this bizarre, dangerous, yet paradoxically wonderful activity—whether it be trimming a second off a slalom gate sequence, squeezing a little more efficiency out of those wing blades or being very scared in a tight West Coast gorge. In writing this guide I hope to give something back to a sport that has given me so much, to enthuse beginners, and re-enthuse those who have been touched by kayaking already.

In the past six years the trickle of whitewater enthusiasts in New Zealand has turned into a flood. Riding that flood, kayaking standards and paradigms have taken a quantum leap forwards, leaving existing river guidebooks in their wake. During the 1994/95 season I began to consider the idea of an up-to-date river guide. At the time I was suffering a dangerous resurgence of enthusiasm for river running after a few years of multi-sport racing. This enthusiasm was mostly for quality, higher grade runs, yet information on how, when and where was frustratingly unavailable. Upon consulting a variety of people in the industry I received the encouragement I needed and dived headfirst into the project. What you are now reading is the proof that whatever you vividly imagine, ardently desire, and enthusiastically act upon will inevitably come to pass.

The nature of the beast in guide books suggests you are not holding a literary giant you'll want to read from cover to cover. In order to achieve objectivity, river descriptions can be painfully dry, but in congruence with my vision of this book I have tried to add spice here and there. This guidebook is your key to the many secrets of Aotearoa wai huka (New Zealand whitewater). It has an unequalled variety of rivers, from the small volume, steep, wilderness runs of the West Coast of the South Island to the stunning waterfall and gorge plunging of the Central North Island. With year-round flows and Kiwi hospitality, New Zealand is a whitewater paradise.

Showcased in the guide are 100 runs ranging in difficulty from class II to class VI. Within the class II category are runs that have outstanding scenery and/or preservation values. There are just too many rivers in New Zealand offering pleasant class I to II float trips to include them all and still keep the whitewater feel of the book. Class III-V runs make up a large part of the New Zealand scene. Beginners and intermediates should still read the 'harder' river descriptions as often there will be a lower put in that offers a worthwhile and less difficult run. This is particularly true in the Buller/West Coast section.

The general layout of the book and within each section is from north to south. If a river has a number of runs or tributaries they will appear top to bottom. The definition of 'great runs' remains mine and may be extracted for the price of a few dark ales after a river trip.

Conservation and preservation of natural resources is a key issue for river runners as we reach the turn of the century. I hope the information contained in this guide will stand as a snapshot of the values and beliefs the whitewater community holds at this point. By virtue of being in-cluded in this book, I consider any of the mentioned runs to be of exceptional value. The individual character of each is only part of the bigger picture that makes Aotearoa wai huka such a valuable resource. Remove any of these runs and the picture becomes fragmented and of less value. It is in everybody's interest to fight for and preserve what we have left. Kayaking and canoesport is not just a weekend adrenal activity, but a vital human development medium for those fortunate to have been touched by it. Two of the best things we can do is have a large group of river users and a written record of use. I hope this book will serve both goals: introduce folk to new river areas and document their use. Let's protect what we have left.

GENERAL INFORMATION

A BEGINNER'S GUIDE TO VITAL STATISTICS

Each river description in this guide features a panel with at-a-glance statistics to help you size up a run. Here's what it all means:

MODERATE
Recommended for novice to intermediate paddlers.

HAIR-RAISING
A commiting trip. Need to be paddling well at class IV and above.

HELICOPTER SHUTTLE
Helicopter access, refer to heli operators and sections at back of book.

RAIN RUN
Requires extra water to bring out full potential.

SHUTTLE DRIVER NEEDED
Logistics are easier if you have a shuttle driver.

OVERNIGHT TRIP
Take your tent.

Class: the ratings in this book are the popularly agreed upon whitewater grades similar to the western United States and Europe. However, it is time to open the grading system out because kayaking standards and thinking have taken a quantum leap forward in the last few years. To this end class VI is a legitimate class. If something gets paddled and is agreed to be harder than class VI+ then it is time for the 'seventh grade'. The 'make my day' grade fills this area. The usual subjective warnings about risks to life and the possibility of dying are not included as this is what has retarded the grading system to date (if you swim in a class VI rapid and don't die, can it be a class VI rapid?). Always remember there are only two type of kayakers: those who swim, and those who are going to swim!

Class I: moving water with a few riffles and small waves. Few or no obstructions.

Class II: easy rapids with waves up to one metre. Clear channels obvious without scouting. The ability to move your craft across the current is not necessary.

Class III: rapids with high irregular waves and narrow passages. The ability to spin and manoeuvre is necessary.

Class IV: difficult rapids requiring a

series of controlled moves, cross-current and spinning in confused water. Scouting often necessary and a reliable roll is mandatory.

Class V: very difficult, long and violent rapids. Nearly always must be scouted. Definite risks in the event of a mishap. Requires a series of controlled, precise, 'must make' moves to navigate successfully.

Class VI: extreme, very dangerous and only for experts. Close inspection is mandatory and all possible safety precautions should be taken.

Make my day: the top end of the grading scale to date. Rather like staring down the barrel of a gun as Clint Eastwood sneers 'you have to ask yourself punk—do you feel lucky?'.

The class information gives the overall difficulty of a river. If only one section in the trip is a harder class then this is noted in brackets ie III (V). (P) indicates a mandatory portage/s.

The whitewater grading system gives a loose impression at best. The + and - ratings add a little more subtlety and depth, but do not indicate the difference between big water and technical, or commitment. (Running a class V rapid on a flooded West Coast river four hours from the nearest vehicle access is very different to a sunny day, roadside, well known class V). Ratings are no substitute for your own judgement.

Level: levels are given as either a gauge reading or in cubic metres per second. They indicate different flows and corresponding changes in difficulty. If the flow is critical to safety this will be noted in the text. (See page 15 for metric/imperial conversions.)

Gauge: also indicates river level in the following ways:

1. Phone numbers of agencies such as NIWA or district/regional councils which monitor river flows.

2. A physical gauge showing levels on the river.

3. The name of the newspaper or other phone which may carry the information.

4. Visual gauge: figure it out yourself. Associated flows are an educated guesstimate.

Length: expressed in kilometres from the put in to the take out.

Gradient: expressed in metres per kilometre. Allowing for the vagaries of the 1:50,000 series maps, the elevation at the take out is subtracted from the elevation at the put in and divided by the length of the run. This

11

only gives the average gradient and can disguise a particularly steep, hard section of water with a long, flat lead-in. Such sections are identified wherever possible and pointed out in the text.

Time: average trip times for recreational kayakers at medium flows—useful information in New Zealand where rivers can flood quickly. If you know bad weather is on the way and you want to fly into a river, it gives you an idea of how much time you have to play with.

Put in: the starting point.

Take out: the finish point. (Many New Zealand rivers have a range of options, so the more common one is indicated here.)
Information on how to find the put in and take out is in the text. Allow for vagaries in given distances.

Shuttle: expressed in kilometres by road from the put in to the take out —**one way**.

Maps: series number of the NZ Topographic 260 series 1:50,000 map which covers the area each river is in. These are an absolute must if you are contemplating a wilderness trip. They will provide information on the locations of nearby huts, tracks or other escape routes should you need them. A copy of the Heinemann's New Zealand Atlas is useful for the big picture and State Highway (SH) numbers.

Character: an attempt to sum up the key characteristics of the run in order to help you choose a trip and add to your knowledge before embarking.

Hot Tip: a particularly useful/less piece of information.

Description: a written picture, a vignette of what to expect on the river in terms of scenery, hazards and points of interest. Rarely will I offer drop by drop descriptions of a run. I believe very much in the adventure aspect of running whitewater. If you **need** someone to spell out how to run the hard rapids you probably shouldn't be there. I am prepared, however, to help you find the put in and take out. Please remember that ownership of this book does not give right of access onto private land.

Ask permission when travelling through other peoples' property and leave all gates and electric fences as you found them.

SAFETY

River safety has done a complete about face in New Zealand in the last five years. From a time when it was uncommon to see throw bags carried on a wilderness trip, we now have one of the safer communities in the world. Rescue life jackets, prussiks, and a host of other equipment are *de rigueur* for many of the river-running community in New Zealand.

I hope this section is redundant as soon as you open the book. The checklist contains the equipment you, or any party should carry on a wilderness river trip (wilderness = more than one hour from easy road access). What you carry with you for a 30 minute trip on a roadside run is up to you, but remember the river does not care that you are an expert —or where you are!

PERSONAL EQUIPMENT

Dry bag	Spare clothing	First aid kit
Spare food	Matches	Insect repellent
Torch	Air bags	Throw rope
Knife or saw	Footwear	Sun screen

Overnight

Sleeping bag	*Plate*	*Utensils*
Soap, toothbrush, etc	*Spare clothing*	

Party Equipment (party of four)

Split paddles x 2	Notebook and pencil

Overnight

Group shelter (tent or fly)	*Stove*	*Cooking utensils*
Food		

Your personal first aid kit should contain: butterfly stitches, antiseptic, painkillers, triangular bandage, strapping bandage, tape, safety pins, absorbent pads, antihistamine tablets and pen and paper.

Spare, dry clothing is a must if you are flying into rivers. New Zealand rivers are 'flashy'. This means they flood quickly and drop quickly. You may be forced to get off the river or, even worse, not actually get on after the helicopter has left! That's when you will be very glad of the spare hat and polypro you threw in at the last moment. Carrying a bivvy bag is not stupid either. If you're forced to spend the night out, having the correct gear will make life more bearable for minimal weight.

Split paddles, throw bag, carabiners, knife, shoes and the knowledge of how to use these things is a pre-requisite. As the m/km rate increases so do the chances of an entrapment or pin. Make sure you know how to deal with such problems. A number of schools and training establishments around the country provide comprehensive programmes in 'hands on' river rescue techniques. One of these courses is a worthwhile investment—your life is worth it.

Before you embark on a trip all members of your team should understand a common set of safety signals.

CAMPING

New Zealand is a camper's paradise. Uncluttered spaces, clean, green and unhassled by the law. It would be very unusual to be woken up at one in the morning by an over-zealous officer of the law and be inspected, inquested, neglected, rejected and finally ordered to leave. There are many stories of such episodes throughout Europe and the US.

This liberal attitude has its drawbacks because it relies on the integrity of campers—that's you. It means that all places should be respected. Here are some simple concepts to help keep the privilege of 'parking up where you want'.

Litter: remove **all** litter when you leave, including food matter. Rats and opossums are a problem in many areas throughout the country.

Fires: there is nothing more annoying than turning up to a camp site only to find four or five fire circles built in the one area—why not just use one? And when you are finished why not toss all the rocks away so other members of *Campus pyromanius* don't happen along and build another one right next to it? Fortunately because of our damp climate camp fires are not an ingrained part of the Kiwi psyche. During summer months many rural authorities impose fire restrictions. These must be adhered to. Fires should be built well away from combustible material and be totally extinguished and destroyed before leaving the area.

Water: New Zealand used to be one of the last remaining countries where you could paddle a river and drink the water as you went. Certainly there are still many rivers where this is the case, but these rivers are dwindling in number. The microscopic organism *Giardia lambia*, more commonly called giardia, has been a recognised problem in New Zealand for the past decade, though it's likely to have been here much longer. If you're concerned about this menace, water should be boiled for five minutes or so before use. A range of filters and chemicals are also available to deal with it. Many people carry drink bottles in their boats and it is wise to fill up bottles at a service station or town if you are camping away from tapped water.

Toileting/washing: When using soap products do not wash yourself or clean dishes directly in rivers, streams, and lakes. To ensure soap products are filtered and broken down before entering a waterbody, it is absolutely imperative that you collect your washing water then move **at least** 20 metres away.

If toilets are unavailable please ensure your toilet deposits aren't left for others to share. Urinate well away from water. Dig a hole (at least through the topsoil) for solid wastes. Use leaf material for wiping, but if you use toilet paper, burn the paper before filling the hole in. Female sanitary protection should be carried out for disposal.

Always leave a campsite in better condition than when you arrived.

CONVERSIONS

New Zealand kayaking has plenty to attract overseas visitors. With this in mind I am very aware of the lack of telemetred flow information and the large number of rivers in this guide which state the gauge as 'visual'. Kayakers and other river users become, by necessity, good at guess-timating river levels. For those used to the US gradients and flow units here are some quick to use conversion tables.

Flow (Cumecs = cubic metres per second, Cfs = cubic feet per second)

Cumecs	Cfs	Cumecs	Cfs	Cumecs	Cfs
2	70	40	1410	140	4940
4	141	50	1765	160	5650
8	280	60	2200	180	6350
12	420	70	2470	200	7060
16	565	80	2820	250	8830
20	700	90	3180	300	10,600
25	880	100	3530		
30	1060	120	4230		

Gradient (Mpk = metres per kilometre, Fpm = feet per mile)

Mpk	Fpm	Mpk	Fpm	Mpk	Fpm
5	26	25	131	45	237
10	52	30	158	50	263
15	80	35	184	55	290
20	105	40	211	60	314

HELICOPTERS

Helicopters are dangerous, however we must deal with them to get to rivers. Understanding helicopter safety rules will ensure your life lasts a lot longer!

1. Stay calm. For some, aviation fumes create symptoms of incompetence: rushing around, slurred speech and the like. A helicopter is a machine just like your car. Treat it as such.

2. Before a helicopter lands ensure all loose items are well away from the rotor wash or stashed under heavier items. Don't wear loose clothing (eg cap) when working around a helicopter.

3. Don't approach the helicopter until the pilot signals. In general, don't do anything around the machine unless you have made eye contact with the pilot beforehand. Always approach from the front. If there is any sort of slope approach from the downhill side.

4. Never walk around the back of the helicopter.

5. Don't tie boats or attach things to the helicopter until given the go ahead from the pilot.

6. When climbing in, leave your life jacket off because it will push you forward off the seat. Be careful not to kick, gouge, rip or shred any instruments. Leave your helmet on.

7. When unloading, if the area is confined and you can't drag your gear away, stockpile it all to one side of the helicopter, crouch over it and wait for the pilot to fly away.

8. Don't do star jumps as a pre-flight warm-up under the rotors!

9. Say Thanks

Helicopter Bake: how to organise a helicopter trip.
A beautiful little dish that brings out the delicate flavours of adventure, fear, excitement, and challenge.
Ingredients:
1 leader - someone to be in charge of phoning the helicopter pilot and

arranging a time and place to be picked up. This person must ensure the team gets to the pick up spot—ahead of time.

1 team of able kayakers. Leave out all those not paddling strongly at the suggested class as these tend to sour the final product.

1 helicopter, usually small and in good order. (Use a 300 for servings of two kayakers, or a 500 for servings of four)

1 pilot. To be well mixed with the helicopter for best results. Pilots need to be used as quickly as possible and will sour if messed around. (Prior to mixing with helicopter verbally agree to a price—cheque or cash—GST inclusive or exclusive and the optimum numbers to keep the price, and not the helicopter, down. A few beers can freshen up a soured pilot if needs be.

1 wad of cash.

1 set of map/s for the area you plan to go into. (see River Information)

1 weather forecast, new and with good news.

1 set of team safety gear. This adds a touch of spice, but will sour a trip rapidly if needed and not included.

To Bake:
Place the team in the correct equipment and mix well with safety gear, maps and weather forecast. Ensure that helicopter and pilot are well mixed and not beaten. Place these two ingredients together and stir in the wad of cash. Preheat the helicopter to operational temperature. Get all people to the river and rinse in water. If in trouble roll and continue. Once all kayakers have been well rinsed get them to a pre-warmed public bar and half bake for two hours. Your trip is done. Serve hot with tall stories, vivid lies, smashing photos and mashed epics. Guaranteed to delight all your guests or frighten your mother.

CHAPTER ONE

NORTHERN NORTH ISLAND

Introducing the northern North Island in a classic whitewater guide is rather like trying to enthuse whitewater paddlers about a 40km flatwater marathon. But seriously folks...

In Northland the time to go paddling is after solid rain. The Mangakahia (near Whangarei, from the bridge on Kaikohe-Donnellys Crossing road), and the Wairua, make up the Northland river contingent.

South of Auckland the Waitetuna (near Raglan), Waitawheta (tributary to Ohinemuri) and possibly even the Pokaiwhenua (near Arapuni) may dish up some surprises for those with adventure in their souls.

Karangahake Gorge (see next page) is the closest whitewater of significance for Auckland paddlers. But, with the general dearth of whitewater in the north, it's little wonder that most Aucklanders have taken over the Wairoa (in Bay of Plenty) and Ngaawapurua (a mere three hours drive away near Taupo) as their local runs. Small wonder too that Aucklanders invade the South Island with such a vengeance during their holidays.

For what it's worth, when stuck in Auckland or Northland do what so many locals do already. GO SURFING! To the south, Raglan has one of the best breaks in the world, and north, there are beaches galore.

OHINEMURI RIVER
KARANGAHAKE GORGE

Proximity to Auckland is one of the best (or worst) features about K' Gorge. Whatever the case this stretch of water has won the hearts of many, and despite its short length and limited whitewater, it remains immensely popular.

The Ohinemuri runs through the spectacular Karangahake Gorge beside SH2 between Waihi and Paeroa. The Gorge has been popular for decades with adventure seekers from the city as it has a river to paddle and some spectacular rock climbing on the cliffs above. With its huge boulders mid river, K' Gorge is unlike many waterways in the north, providing not only interesting whitewater, but also a playground for practising eddy turns and other stuff!

This run is worth a visit if you're passing and there's been plenty of rain in the last 48 hours. From the Owharoa put in the first few kilometres are easy class I-II water. The action begins just above the township of Karangahake with a drop into class III+ (only at high flow) bouldery rapids. This is the start of a kilometre of fun whitewater down to the take out.

CLASS:	II+ to III+
LEVEL:	needs quite a lot of rain
GAUGE:	visual
LENGTH:	5.5km
GRADIENT:	6.5m/km (most of the drop happens in the last kilometre)
TIME:	1-3 hours
PUT IN:	Owharoa Falls parking area (or anywhere else along the road that offers access)
TAKE OUT:	at the old rail bridge 800m below the Karangahake township
SHUTTLE:	5.5km
MAPS:	NZ Topo T13
CHARACTER:	close to Auckland
HOT TIP:	wait for the rain - lots of it!

To get to the put in: Owharoa Falls is about 1km east of the township of Waikino. Park and find the easiest way down to the water. If you don't want to paddle the top section there are many other possible put in spots as you drive down the gorge.

The take out is where the walkway through an old tunnel comes out on the road, about 800m east of Karangahake.

CHAPTER TWO

EAST CAPE/BAY OF PLENTY/WAIKATO RIVER

If you're looking for an area with a multitude of rivers, East Cape's rugged ranges, Bay of Plenty's gorges and shimmering lakes, and the mighty Waikato River will satisfy the most discerning connoisseurs of whitewater.

Bay of Plenty is steeped in Maori tradition for it was here that two of the first canoes bearing Polynesian explorers from far off Hawaiki are said to have made landfall. Led by Tamatekapua, the Arawa canoe landed at Maketu and his crew travelled up the Kaituna River, reaching Lakes Rotoiti and Rotorua. The Kaituna remains a river of deep spiritual and historical significance for the Arawa people, and we have them to thank that it still flows the clear green it does today—in the early 1980s, the Arawa tribe prevented Rotorua District Council from discharging the city's sewage down the river by fighting the proposal right through to the Waitangi Tribunal, and winning.

Whether for industry, energy, recreation or adventure tourism, Bay of Plenty and neighbouring Waikato contains some of the most heavily exploited sections of water in the country. Once long and uninterrupted transport routes for Maori and Europeans, many of the rivers here are are now dammed and controlled for hydroelectric generation. Despite this, rivers here, particularly the Wairoa, Kaituna, Rangitaiki and upper Waikato, remain a playground for paddlers. The climate is moderate, and paddling is viable year-round.

In general the rivers here are small volume (less than 30 cumecs) with the exception of the Waikato, New Zealand's longest river, which flows between 50 and 300 cumecs. In a region dominated by volcanic activity, the Rangitaiki, Waikato, Kaituna and Wairoa have all cut their way through old volcanic ignimbrite deposits, hence their steep-walled pool-drop nature, especially the latter two.

The Waikato River once sported rapids from Taupo to Karapiro, but in
the 1930s a grand scheme was devised to harness the swiftly falling
water for electricity. The Waikato is now controlled, from the gates at
Lake Taupo through a series of eight dams to Karapiro, and little remains of what must have been an incredible stretch of whitewater. What
does remain is still incredible. Aratiatia, released three times a day, is as
yet unpaddled—a deadly yet beautiful maelstrom of whitewater. Huka
Falls is a rapid regarded with awe by most paddlers, although an
increasing number of paddlers are adding the Fall's notch to their
paddles. Huka has had its share of victims, one of the earliest being a
hostile visitor to a local chief. The chief challenged the visitor to a race
down the falls, but just as their canoes reached the brink, the chief
grabbed a flax rope thrown by his warriors who hauled him to safety.
Given that going over the Huka was regarded as fatal, he must have had
great faith in the rope throwing skills of his men.

Remote East Cape is separated from the Bay of Plenty by the largest
continuous tract of native forest in the North Island—Urewera National
Park and Raukumara Forest Park. Life in East Cape moves with a pace
all of its own. Likewise, its two major rivers, the Motu and Mohaka, are
aloof and run their course without the hubbub of human interaction.
Both have a wilderness feel and both are long enough to offer multi-day
kayaking trips. The Motu flows to the coast north of the cape, while the
Mohaka forms the southern boundary of East Cape region. Both have
come under pressure from the hydroelectricity industry. The Motu
escaped with a conservation order in the 1970s—the first river in New
Zealand protected for its wild and scenic values.

East Cape rivers have sliced their way through old sediments deposited when New Zealand was below the sea, 777 million years ago during
the Oligocene epoch. Layer upon layer of sandstone, siltstone, mudstone
and limestone formed as the land dipped beneath the waves of the
Oligocene coastline. These same sequences were repeated in reverse
when the land rose again. The region's climate is controlled by its
mountains. Rain is dumped heavily in northerly frontal systems, but
long settled periods in summer can lower river levels dramatically.

This chapter features the best river runs on offer in these regions, but
if you are well travelled, well kayaked, or simply want to do something
different, try the Tarawera River, which originates in Lake Tarawera and
flows through Kawerau. There's also the Whirinaki River near Murupara,
with its lovely scenery and water (in good flows). For tough adventure

kayaking, organise or get on a trip into the Te Hoe River (which flows into the Mohaka). The lower Kaituna has some out-of-control hair boating. Gisborne paddlers have some well kept secrets in that part of the country although you need to ply them with all manner of beverages to get the local information out of them.

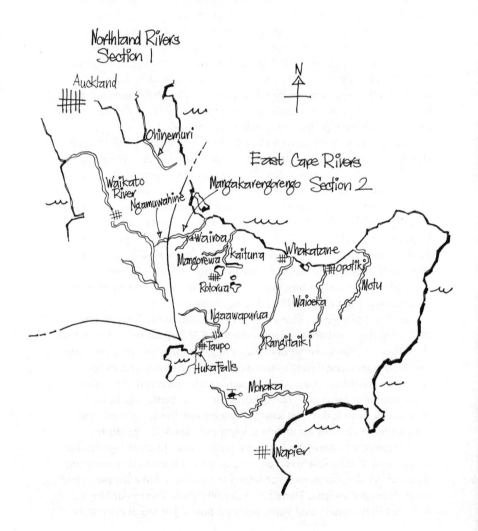

WAIROA RIVER

The Wairoa is a classic short run and the local river for Aucklanders, being a mere two-and-a-half hours' drive from that whitewater desert. Dammed for electricity generation, the river is released down its original bed just 26 days a year for the benefit of rafters and paddlers. We owe that to a group of kayakers who fought for the river when the dam was built by Kaimai Energy. A list of release dates is issued at the start of each summer. The water is turned on at 10am then off at 4pm. Because it's so short, most parties do the run a few times a day. Contact a local kayak club or any of the rafting companies if you need the flow dates. The gauge for the Wairoa is on river left 20m below the MacLaren Falls Bridge.

Fun play holes and waves warm up the muscles for 800m before you are full-on into it. Mother's Nightmare has a tricky entrance followed by a series of pillow rocks down its 50m length. Run the final drop hard right. A pleasant pool leads to a class III even gradient rock garden with some good play holes in it. Below here is Double Trouble and Mushroom.

CLASS:	IV+ V
LEVEL:	class IV+: 12 cumecs class V: >20 cumecs
GAUGE:	water flowing level with the old AA road sign at the put in means a 'normal' (12 cumecs) flow, if you can't see it the flow is high, if it's out of the water it is low!
LENGTH:	2.7km
GRADIENT:	15m/km
TIME:	1 hour
PUT IN:	MacLaren Falls Bridge 1km off SH29
TAKE OUT:	Substation, SH29
SHUTTLE:	3km
MAPS:	NZ Topo U14
CHARACTER:	steep, technical, tight bedrock gorge
HOT TIP:	warm water FUN

Another pool leads to the top of Devil's Elbow—a slightly more complex rapid with a couple of moves to make before the boof into the final hole.

This puts you in the pool above the Waterfall, which can be portaged on the right if desired. Run the initial V-wave on the right and eddy out, or immediately cross hard left to avoid the Toaster just before the 3m Waterfall.

The Rollercoaster has a couple of entry options including a sneak route. These can be scouted from the right using the ropes to gain access to the ledges at the bottom. The water flows into a nasty undercut cliff at the bottom. There is a save-yourself rope hanging down the cliff, but best not go near enough to need it. Those portaging need to paddle across the pool to river left and run their boats hard up onto a rock between two drops. Someone on the rock to catch a nose-loop is reassuring.

Things ease off through some smaller drops, flat water and into the class II+ Rock Garden down to the slalom rapid. Beginners can walk and paddle upriver to the small, but well used, wave at the bottom of the Rock Garden. Either take out by the Kaimai Whitewater Club's clubrooms or continue on for another kilometre, which includes a couple of class III rapids and 2m waterfall to the power station.

Having someone who knows the river helps as a horizon line is often all you will see until committed to many of the drops.

To get to the put in: find the signposted turnoff to MacLaren Falls about 25km west of Tauranga on SH29. Drive down to the bridge. Put in on the right 30m below the MacLaren Falls Bridge, behind the power house.

To get to the take out: back on SH29, drive 3km to a power substation and park.

MacLaren Falls is being run more and more by paddlers looking for more challenge. It weighs in at around class V+. Good luck and make sure you get a photo!!

The Mangakarengorengo River is the left bank tributary joining the Wairoa just upstream of the MacLaren Falls Bridge. This is a fun class IV run, possible only in high flow, but needs a fair bit of rain in the ranges. It gets more serious in big flood. There is one difficult fall in this stretch— a probable portage for many. Watch out for it at the bottom of a rapid. Put in where SH29 crosses the river.

The Ngamuwahine which crosses under SH29 10km north of the Wairoa put in is also runnable at high water levels and rafting companies will sometimes go there if the Wairoa is too high. Put in up Ngamuwahine Rd and take out at the SH29 bridge of the same name. Class III-IV+.

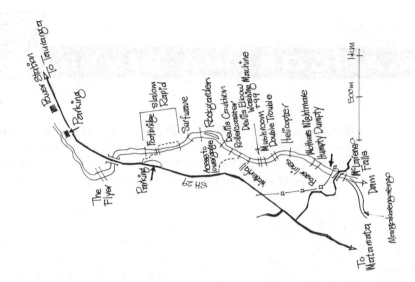

MANGOREWA RIVER

The Mangorewa River crosses the old coach road that links Rotorua and Taupo. Mostly it's no more than a trickle of water linking a series of swimming holes in the most amazing scenery imaginable. But after a decent night's rain the river turns into something resembling a half pipe for kayakers.

CLASS:	III-IV+
LEVEL:	needs rain to put in at Pyes Pa Rd (a solid night should do it)
GAUGE:	visual
LENGTH:	34km
GRADIENT:	10m/km
TIME:	5-8 hours
PUT IN:	Pyes Pa Rd or through Lemprieres Farm, 1601 Te Matai Rd. Phone 07 573 8034
TAKE OUT:	Maungarangi Rd off SH33 near Long Ridge Park
SHUTTLE:	40km
MAPS:	NZ Topo U15
CHARACTER:	steepsided gorge similar to the Kaituna
HOT TIP:	always be looking ahead and scouting for trees across the river

From the Pyes Pa Rd put in the river starts out shallow and fast with a smooth flat bottom and a range of easy waterfalls. One larger fall, about an hour from the put in is normally portaged. After this fall the gradient starts to pick up a little, the walls close in and the river starts to look like its neighbouring cousin, the Kaituna. Most rapids can be scouted from your boat or the banks but there are a couple of blind gorges which offer no chance of scouting. Care must be taken to avoid logs.

About 10km down, the water volume increases because of the natural springs in the river at this point. The water gushing from the rocks on both sides of the river is quite impressive and also allows this part of the river to be run year round. It is possible to gain access to the river through the Lemprieres Farm. For a small koha (donation) they will run you the couple of kilometres down the farm track on a tractor to the river.

Just below the springs are two of the biggest falls on the river. The first is at the bottom of a steep rapid. In low flows you may want to portage on river left, in higher flows it can be run on river right. The second happens a hundred metres downstream. This one is exciting because there's no opportunity to scout or portage, but a good boof off the right side will see you safely in the eddy. A few more small drops keep the interest up until the gradient sits right down. This leaves quite a few kilometres of flat paddling down to the Kaituna confluence, then a short paddle *up* the Kaituna to Long Ridge Park. There are higher take out points but you will need to negotiate your own access to these if you know any of the farmers in the area. In researching the book none of the farmers wanted to have their land published as an access point.

To get to the put in: from Rotorua head around the lake through the settlement of Ngongotaha. About five kilometres north of the township is the turnoff to Tauranga on Pyes Pa Rd. Follow this road for about 16km until it drops into a deep gorge—this is the Mangorewa.

To get to the take out: there are a couple of options and it doesn't make a lot of difference. Either take Te Matai Rd through to Te Puke then head back south. Or go back to SH33 past the Kaituna River and head north on this. What you are looking for is Maungarangi Rd off SH33 about 2km south of Paengaroa. Once at this road go 900m down to Long Ridge Park just before the Kaituna River bridge. Access the river via the park.

Donald Calder

KAITUNA RIVER
OKERE FALLS RUN

Only those in river craft see the full beauty of the upper Kaituna, the outlet of lakes Rotorua and Rotoiti, famous for its waterfalls, play spots and its magical deep, green gorge. The Kaituna is fun, good for the soul, and a must if you are in the area and like to plunge off steep ledges and waterfalls. This run (including Okere Falls) has only become popular after commercial rafting began in 1992. Since then it has become one of the most exploited runs in the North Island.

The river starts at the slalom course below the control gates and winds its way into a bush-fringed gorge. A concrete portal—the remains of an old power station—splits the river. Go right. This is a 2.5m waterfall (Okere Falls) into an aerated pool. At the bottom of the pool is The Weir. Boof hard into the eddy on the right. This rather simple looking hydraulic is capable of flipping rafts and holding people for some time.

Tutea's Falls, when you get to it, is obvious. From the cliff-bound eddy above, the horizon drops away, but a well-timed launch, hard right, gives a clean landing and almost dry face. Many, however, crash down the middle and get turned over before rolling up to the cheers of the spectators on the viewing gallery. Take this waterfall seriously. At lower flows (200 or less) some people are pushed to the bottom of the river, grazing knuckles, breaking ribs, noses and paddles. Even boogie boarders have been pinned to the bottom for longer than comfortable periods.

CLASS:	III-IV
LEVEL:	200-500 on the gates. (200 = three gates at 200, 500 = three gates at 500 and so on)
GAUGE:	at the put in
LENGTH:	1.1km
GRADIENT:	36m/km
TIME:	30-60 minutes
PUT IN:	control gates by the Kaituna River Bridge on SH33
TAKE OUT:	last drop above Trout Pool Falls (don't miss it)
SHUTTLE:	1.2km
MAPS:	NZ Topo U15
CHARACTER:	small volume waterfalls and drops
HOT TIP:	Okere Falls is one of the best BOOFS in the country.

Below the falls are seven more class III drops. You can carry down Hinemoa's Steps and put in below the falls if you wish. All the drops have potential for enders and side surfing, but the last is where most of the action is. With warm water and a very friendly play hole, you can spend hours here working on your aerial manoeuvres. If you just want a play session, it is possible to put in right at the last hole. Below this drop is Trout Pool Falls. This has claimed a couple of lives and broken a kayaker's ankles, but also been run on numerous occasions—be warned.

Access is a delicate issue here. Please respect the mana of the local iwi who regard the river and its surrounds as a deeply spiritual and significant place. Don't bash through the bush along the gorge. Use amenities

at all times. Please be discreet when changing as nudity offends and gives the sport a bad name.

Flows are read off the control gates immediately above the put in. Each of the three gates is numbered in divisions of 100 (equal to 3 cumecs). Therefore three gates at 300 equals 27 cumecs. When talking about flows people refer to one number which is what all three of the gates will be at. Rafting companies operate between 200-500. Below 200, kayaks can hit the bottom of the falls hard. Above 500 is okay, but the river is fast and pushy. It is kayaked with fully open gates above 1300.

To get to the put in: find the small settlement of Okere Falls about 21km north of Rotorua on SH33. The carpark and put in are 500m north of the Okere Falls Store just before the Kaituna River Bridge. Put in 30 metres below the control gates.

To get to the take out: drive 1.2km down the road opposite the put in carpark, signposted Troutpool Rd, Okere Falls. Make sure your car is locked and all valuables removed or well hidden.

RANGITAIKI RIVER
JEFFS JOY RUN

A river that epitomises Kiwi creativity in naming rapids. Where else can you find such superlative describers of features like 'rock A' and 'rock B'. The people who named these were not out to help guidebook writers that's for sure! Imagine being told to float downstream and watch out for rock A! Strange but true.

The Rangitaiki is a great run for paddlers looking to cut their teeth on lots of class III water with the added excitement of one class IV drop. In fact, this is probably where a majority of the North Island paddlers run their first class IV rapid. The run has lovely scenery, continuous class II-III rapids and is long enough to really sink your blades into. (see map on page 34)

Having diced with death on the forest roads into the put in, unwind through the first 200m of flat water to the top of the slalom site—scene of New Zealand's first and only World Cup Slalom event in 1991. The first of the rapids is the home of rock A and rock B—see if you can spot them! The whitewater eases a little for about 150m before Fantail Falls and Jeff's Joy.

CLASS:	III+ (IV) IV
LEVEL:	class III+ (IV): <30 cumecs class IV: >30 cumecs
GAUGE:	flow from NIWA Rotorua 07 346 1950, ask for the flow at Murupara
LENGTH:	11.5km
GRADIENT:	9m/km
TIME:	2.5-5 hours
PUT IN:	end of the access road
TAKE OUT:	at the rafting finish area
SHUTTLE:	10.5km
MAPS:	NZ Topo V17
CHARACTER:	single channel, even gradient rapids, bush and forest-lined banks
HOT TIP:	don't try to walk out

These can be inspected by exiting on river right and grovelling down amongst the toetoe (native cutty grass that slices things) to the viewing point.

Things happen quickly once you drop down the steep ramp of Fantail Falls. There are a couple of eddies on river right to take a break before the plunge over Jeff's Joy, but they are small and will not take more than two boats. From here the main line is left of centre and watch out for the wall at the bottom.

Jeff's Joy was named after Jeff, surprisingly enough, whose surname has eluded me. Jeff was a tyre-tuber of great repute who worked in the forests around Murupara. He accompanied one of the first trips down this section in the early 1970s. Apparently he tubed down this stretch, but by the time he got to the final hole of this rapid, (now Jeff's Joy) he was unconscious from the beating he sustained on the way from Fantail Falls. His mates duly revived him and he lived to tell the tale not to mention have a rapid named after him. Long live Jeff.

A big pool and recirculating eddy at the bottom of Jeff's Joy is a handy place to re-group, collect gear, and repair damaged egos. From here is a kilometre of class II-III water to the 'flat stretch'—another startling adjectival explanation. This is where paddlers interested in the class II-III delights of the lower run get on (see put in description and map). The lower section is a fun, challenging run for intermediate paddlers and contains many rapids so I won't single any out. Be aware that getting to the side in the Rangitaiki is difficult because of bushes and toetoe. This makes rescuing and reacquainting swimmers with their equipment tricky. Always keep an eye out for new trees in the river. Rafting companies use the river regularly and are a good source of information regarding new hazards in the river.

To get to the take out: turn off SH5 between Rotorua and Taupo towards Murupara. Just before the Rangitaiki river bridge (at Murupara) turn right onto a gravel road marked Low Level Rd just next to the Forest Information Centre. After 800m this forks—take the right fork. A further 300m sees the junction with Kiorenui Rd (sealed). Turn left. Drive 1.7km to a sign indicating Rangitaiki River Access on the left. About 600m along this road it forks, take the left fork down to the river, picnic area and take out area. Murupara to the take out is 3.7km.

To get to the put in: return to Kiorenui Rd and turn left. After 2km the road turns to gravel. At 7km from the take out is a road signposted Tautika Rd/Rangitaiki River. This is the access road for people interested in the bottom section only. The carpark is 3.3km down the dirt road. A further 300m past Tautika Rd is Ngahuringa Rd and the route to the upper put in. Stay left at any major junctions and drive 3km down to the river.

RANGITAIKI RIVER
ANIWHENUA RUN

This section of the Rangitaiki below Aniwhenua is one of the best novice trips in this region, though in 1995 Bay Of Plenty Electricity launched a bid to dam the gorge up to the base of Aniwhenua. River users and environmental groups banded together to form *Rangitaiki No More Dams* to fight the proposal, which was still under appeal in 1996.

Aniwhenua Falls makes the put in an exciting moment. Kayakers have been plummeting off these falls for years. There are only two things you don't want to do. Don't turn sideways in the narrow approach channel, or turn upside down just before the drop. Otherwise the falls have been paddled in every manner possible by complete novices to mega-gods. Whatever you do, take plenty of photos.

Below Aniwhenua the river flows between fantastic walls of ancient volcanic ash. The water is mostly class I-II with excellent waves for aspiring surf pigs. When flows are good the rocks are well covered, producing good waves, pools and places for novices to relax or practise eddy turns and rolls.

To get to the put in: from the township of Murupara head east 2km to the turnoff signposted Whakatane, Te Teko, Kouriki.

CLASS:	II
LEVEL:	20-40 cumecs
GAUGE:	NIWA Rotorua 06 346 1950. Ask for the flow below Aniwhenua Dam
LENGTH:	8km
GRADIENT:	3m/km
TIME:	3-4 hours
PUT IN:	below Aniwhenua Falls, or paddle the falls
TAKE OUT:	where the road first returns to the river 7km from the Aniwhenua Power Station turn off.
SHUTTLE:	9.5km
MAPS:	NZ Topo V16
CHARACTER:	single channel, excellent gorge scenery.
HOT TIP:	an absolute beauty for novice paddlers

Follow this road for 3.5km to another junction. Turn left and follow the Galatea Road for just over 20km. Turn left at a road signposted Black Rd, Aniwhenua Power Station, cross the dam to the road end by the power station.

To get to the take out: drive back out to Galatea Rd and turn left. Follow this road for about 7km to where the road drops to within metres of the river. There are a couple of small tracks down to the water.

It is possible to extend the trip by continuing to the bridge at Lake Matahina. This adds another 5-6km and is mostly flat water through farmland.

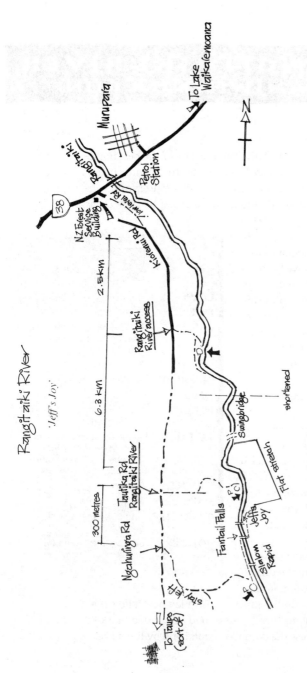

Rangitaiki River-
Jeff's Joy run (page 31)

WAIOEKA RIVER

The Waioeka has two excellent easy and scenic day trips for visitors to the East Cape area. The top section makes an excellent overnight trip for those wanting the adventure experience. To kayak the upper section it's best to run the Koranga stream (one of the main tributaries of the Waioeka) from the end of the road to Moanui Station, on the boundary of the magnificent Urewera National Park. It takes about one and a half hours to paddle down to the Waioeka/Koranga confluence. The Koranga itself is fun with steep and tight rock-garden rapids, all of which can be boat scouted. The most difficult rapid is about 100m above the confluence, a small waterfall that runs into a cliff on river right.

Once at the Waioeka Forks the action eases for an hour or so of open shingle type rapids. The river then picks up with numerous rocky rapids and chutes all within the class III realm. The best take out is on Wairata Rd, an access route to the Urewera.

The second run, known as Hells Gate is from just below Wairata, off SH2. The rapids are all class I-II+ and don't require inspection. Although it flows alongside the road, this river still has a wilderness feel about it with plenty to offer novice and intermediate paddlers. Both runs gain a half to full class more when in flood.

CLASS:	I - III
LEVEL:	needs a good dousing of rain
GAUGE:	visual
LENGTH:	28.5km
GRADIENT:	5m/km
TIME:	5-8 hours, or do it over two days
PUT IN:	on the Moanui Valley Rd, by a footbridge where the road first meets the river
TAKE OUT:	junction of Wairata Rd and SH2
SHUTTLE:	40km
MAPS:	NZ Topo W16, W17
CHARACTER:	wilderness, remote trip with excellent water when running high
HOT TIP:	try it, you might like it

To get to the put in: find the turnoff to Koranga and the Moanui Valley off SH2 about 9km east of Matawai, (or 60 km southeast of Opotiki). Turn onto this gravel road. In less than a kilometre the road forks. Take the right fork and follow signs along Moanui Valley Rd. This road winds down alongside Moanui Stream. Just as it meets the Koranga River proper is a swingbridge. Park and get in here. There are other put in options further along the road, but after a kilometre it climbs away from the river again.

To get to the take out: With plenty of water in the river you can paddle to the Waioeka River/SH2 junction at Wairata (about 41km south of Opotiki). If the water is low, or you just can't be bothered, it is possible to cut the trip shorter by turning off SH2 at Wairata and driving about 4km up the gravel road to any point available for disembarkation. Just before Okurata Stream is probably the last place to take out.

MOTU RIVER

Jump at any opportunity to get on a trip down the Motu. Bush and gorge scenery, good camping and enjoyable whitewater all feature on one of the North Island's rare multi-day trips. The shuttle is difficult to organise, but once on the river any hassles are quickly forgotten. Unless, of course, you realise after four hours on the water you left the shuttle car keys at the top— yes, it happened.

CLASS:	III-IV
LEVEL:	30-150 cumecs
GAUGE:	measured at the take out. Flow information available from NIWA Rotorua 07 346 1950
LENGTH:	88.5km
GRADIENT:	5m/km
TIME:	2-4 days
PUT IN:	2km past Motu Falls
TAKE OUT:	road bridge on SH35
SHUTTLE:	146km
MAPS:	NZ Topo X15 and X16
CHARACTER:	single channel, stunning scenery, alternating bedrock gorges and deep bush valley
HOT TIP:	practise your firelighting skills if rain is forecast

The trip is usually done in three comfortable days, but during very high flows has been paddled in a day. A hut at Otipi is used by rafting groups as a put in spot and/or overnight location. The upper gorge to Otipi is 34.5km. Otipi to the SH35 bridge is 54km.

The whitewater action is in the gorge sections. Each gorge has a different style of rapid. Upper gorge rapids have short and tight drops among sharp, angled, greywacke bedrock. The two of note are Bullivant's Cascade and Motu Slot. The upper section, with its narrow single channels, tends to trap logs and wood so watch out.

Steeper, harder rapids flowing through large rounded boulders are the flavour of the lower gorge. Of note are The Hump, less than a kilometre into the gorge, Double Staircase just over halfway through, and Helicopter Rapid just above the confluence with the Te Kahika Stream. There is an excellent camping spot at this junction. Portaging is no problem unless the river is flowing higher than 150 cumecs and the river's banks are covered.

When organising a trip on the Motu, don't enter either of the gorges late in the afternoon or early evening. Once in the gorges campsites are almost non-existent and you could end up sitting the night out on an uncomfortable rock ledge. Campsites on other sections of the river are plentiful and require either some knowledge of the established sites or an eye for a sheltered, comfy little haven to spend the night. A tent fly is the usual form of shelter and you can either build fires or take a small stove to cook on. I recommend the small stove option in case rain dampens your campsite and the firewood supply. To date there are no reports of giardia, nevertheless boiling drinking water is a healthy precaution.

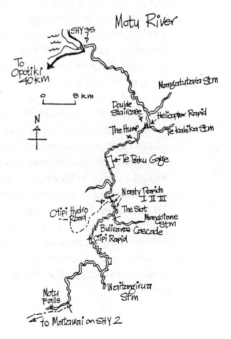

The country around the Raukumara Range, through which the river flows, is remote and rugged. It is easy to see why this was the last area in the country to be mapped. Keep this in mind if you choose to leave your split paddles behind or fail to screen the skills of the people in your team!

The history of the Motu is almost as spectacular as the scenery. The first European exploration of the Motu river area was in December 1879 when surveyor Alfred Teasdale and two Maori helpers surveyed the western boundary of the Mangatu block. By February 1880 they had reached Te Paku near Mangakirikiri and continued on to Rutatahi .

On February 10, 1919 four locals

from Matawai made what is believed to be the first descent of the Motu. They set off in two wooden boats and emerged ten harrowing days later with only one. In 1935 the second known descent was made by a party of three in a 5m flat-bottomed punt with a sheet of flatiron nailed underneath for protection against rocks. For 10 days they battled the river before reaching the coast.

A party of three under the leadership of Kahu Bullivant made the third descent in 1953. Bullivant's Cascade was named on this trip after Kahu was stranded on the rocks without his craft and had to jump in and swim to catch up. Their rubber dinghy was caught in a flood and they rode the river to the coast in only three days. From 1957 there has been constant activity on the Motu. Until the early 1970s descents were feasible only to those with access to war surplus inflatable dinghies. Kayakers and commercial rafting came next, and since the introduction of plastic kayaks in the early 1980s, the river trip has been made possible for many.

The Motu has been thoroughly wrung through the hydroelectric wringer. During the 1970s, through the efforts of Graham Eggar and John Mackay, the campaign to save the Motu from hydro development was launched. By encouraging as many trips as possible down the river they gave impetus to the *Save the Rivers* campaign. The end of the 1970s saw most of the environmental groups in the country supporting the preservation of the Motu. In 1981 the environmental movement won 'wild and scenic rivers protection' for the Motu, the first river to be so classified in New Zealand. It is important we remember the history and battles for these rivers so that we understand what must be dealt with to ensure our remaining natural waterways are protected.

To get to the put in: from Opotiki drive south on SH2 through the Waioeka Gorge to Matawai, a distance of 77km. If coming via Gisborne just follow SH2 to Matawai. Turn left onto Motu Rd and follow it for 23km to Motu Falls. It is possible to put in here though most continue to Waitangirua Station (check with the farmer first), and get a few kilometres down the farm road. Put in anywhere with river access.

To get to the take out: from Opotiki head east on SH35 approx 44km to the Motu road bridge. The usual take out is on river right under the bridge.

MOHAKA RIVER
UPPER RUN

Here's one for you. If you are after a fun, relaxing, thoroughly enjoyable weekend away I recommend the upper section of the Mohaka. The super bonus on this one is some of the nicest wilderness hot pools in New Zealand.

CLASS:	III
LEVEL:	any, but after some rain is better
GAUGE:	visual
LENGTH:	45km
GRADIENT:	5m/km
TIME:	2-3 days
PUT IN:	below Mangatanguru Stream
TAKE OUT:	McVicar Rd, just above SH5 bridge
SHUTTLE:	Helicopter Section 2
MAPS:	NZ Topo U19, U20, V20
CHARACTER:	beautiful deep-sided wilderness valley, excellent whitewater through mid section
HOT TIP:	exactly what you'll feel like after soaking and camping at the Mangatainoka hot springs

Picture this: you've just paddled a couple of hours of scenic class II water, you've set up camp, poured the wine and broken out the cheese and crackers. Then you climb onto the decking around the pools, choose the pool you want according to temperature, and lower your stressed (from city life) bones into the clean, hot water. A bellbird choruses from the rimu forest. Perfect! This is one of kayaking's best kept secrets, but now you have the knowledge.

Most trips start with a helicopter dropoff just below Mangatanguru stream (there are access problems higher up because of private property). A couple of lazy class II hours will see you at the hot pools, though you'll need to keep close contact with the map as the hot pools area is not obvious from the river. You can do a longer day and camp lower but the hot pools make a great spot to park up for a long night of decadence.

The class III whitewater begins a kilometre or so below the pools. This continues for an hour or so before easing to class II as you exit the gorge and see farmland for the first time just before the bridge at Ripia. It's possible to use this as a put in but there is a complex set of gravel roads to access the area.

Once clear of the farmland you enter another class II gorge section; the fishing and scenery is world class, the camping is superb—this section makes a great trip on its own. This last stretch, from the Ripia bridge to the McVicars take out, is 21km.

To get to the helicopter pick up (if you use the Poronui Station operator: from the lakefront in Taupo, drive 26km along SH5 towards Napier. Turn right at Taharua Rd, also marked as access to Clements Rd, Kaimanawa Forest. Drive 22km to Heli Sika at Poronui Station. Ensure you have a shuttle driver!

To get to the take out: the take out is on a gravel bar at the end of McVicars Rd, one kilometre west of the SH5 bridge over the Mohaka 85km from Taupo.

The section below the SH5 bridge is a fun beginner's trip with straightforward class I-II rapids and great scenery. It is about 8km to the first take out point.

MOHAKA RIVER
TE HOE TO WILLOW FLAT RUN

This section of the Mohaka was pioneered by Pelham Housego and his mates back in 1970. It has been one of the North Island's long standing great runs marred only by the complexity and length of the shuttle. You really need to shanghai a driver for this one.

CLASS:	III+ (IV) IV
LEVEL:	class III+ (IV): 25-80 cumecs class IV: >80 cumecs
GAUGE:	visual
LENGTH:	14km
GRADIENT:	6.5m/km
TIME:	3-6 hours
PUT IN:	Te Hoe Station
TAKE OUT:	Willow Flat Bridge
SHUTTLE:	22.5km (gravel road)
MAPS:	NZ Topo V19
CHARACTER:	huge boulder gardens, even gradient, siltstone canyon
HOT TIP:	one of the North Island's best one day wilderness trips

Once bidding your friendly driver a fond farewell, and praying that they make it out again, you push off into a nice three kilometres of class II water, a great warm-up for the first gorge which contains the crux rapid of the run. This first gorge announces itself with a narrowing of the river and some huge conglomerate blocks which obstruct your view. Some easy manoeuvring around these opens up the lead in to Long Rapid (a sidestream entering on the right via a spectacular waterfall just below the rapid also verifies your position). This rapid starts on river right with some dodging of holes, followed by a cross back to the left side, then just stay out of trouble down to the bottom.

Having dispensed with this rapid settle back to a good few kilometres of nice class II and III moves in a stunning sedimentary rock canyon. A section of single braid riffles leads into the next gorge. The Sharks Fin and Pencil Sharpener live here. Both have been tempered by age and pack only some of the punch they used to a decade ago due to the susceptibility of the siltstones in this gorge to erosion and collapse. This run used to be considered IV-V but many of the difficult rapids have almost completely eroded away. In 1988 a rafting group were in the gorge when an earthquake shook the area and the water around them suddenly dried up. The guides figured that a big slip had come into the river somewhere behind them and dammed the river, so they climbed to high ground and waited in case the dam gave way. Apparently all that was left were pools crammed with stranded fish and eels. A few hours later water started trickling through as the dam gradually released. Slip Rapid was the result, a class V proposition when it was first run. Now it's a class II+ boulder dodge, such is the speedy erosion in this canyon.

The final gorge is a maze of enormous limestone boulders that really keeps the suspense up. Some nice play holes can be found as you weave your way through these. The size of the boulders continues to increase and just when you think they can't get bigger, Hotel Rock appears—aptly named as this is about the size of it. Shortly after passing Hotel Rock (and doing the customary headshake as you try figuring out where this monster came from) you'll spy the Willow Flat bridge and the take out.

To get to the take out: this is no easy task. You need to get on SH2 between Napier and Wairoa. About 57km north of the Napier-Taupo Rd/ SH2 junction look for an AA sign to Willow Flat. Thirteen kilometres of gravel road take you to the bridge and the take out on the river right side down a small road 800m back from the bridge.

To get to the put in: cross the Willow Flat bridge and follow the gravel road about 12km to Haliburton Rd. Turn left and drive a further 7.5km to another fork, turn left by the white letterbox. Continue another 3km down to the Haliburton's Farm. It is customary and good manners to stop in and ask permission to cross their land to get to the river. Phoning beforehand is essential: 06 839 1666. A koha of some sort is also appreciated. Fresh fruit is a good idea as these folk are a long way from the nearest store. A 2km farm track leads you down to the river's edge. Be careful in wet weather as a normal town vehicle will not make it up the farm track in slippery conditions.

WAIKATO RIVER
NGAAWAPURUA RAPID

Ngaawapurua means waters turning over on themselves. Whether this refers to the wave or the eddies on the side, no one is sure. Whatever the 'true' definition, it's still New Zealand's most surfed wave and played-in rapid, cause of 'wide eye syndrome' for novice paddlers, site of numerous slaloms (two national championships), and the annual National Whitewater Rodeo Champs. This is where you go to strut your stuff or get stuffed while strutting! See if you can one up Ralph in his C1 who has been outclassing K1 paddlers for the last ten years. Or try Donald Johnstone's 1993 rodeo stunt of surfing while sitting on the back deck, then standing up in the cockpit. You name it and it's likely to have been done. This is a place not to be missed.

CLASS:	II+
LEVEL:	any
GAUGE:	ECNZ Flow Phone 0800 820 082 (flow below Aratiatia)
LENGTH:	n/a
GRADIENT:	n/a
TIME:	as long as you want
PUT IN:	at the rapid
TAKE OUT:	where you put in
SHUTTLE:	0
MAPS:	NZ Topo U17
CHARACTER:	big water surfing
HOT TIP:	one of *the* greatest play spots in New Zealand

When the water is big, the surfing is huge. Between 150-300 cumecs is where the surf action lies. Two huge eddies on either side return you to striking distance of the front wave for another bout of surf or submarine. Surfing at flows below 150 cumecs is not so hot, but a rock pour-over can provide some good retendo moves at the top of the rapid.

To get to Ngaawapurua: the turnoff to Ngaawapurua is off SH5 about 12km north of Taupo. The turn off is signposted National Equestrian Centre and Aratiatia dam. After 3km, at another sign for the National Equestrian Centre, take a left. Go past the centre and turn right down a dirt road signposted Ngaawapurua Scenic Reserve. Follow this road about 3km to its end. It is possible to put in the river at a number of sites along the dirt road. This gives a great class I-II+ run down to Ngaawapurua through some whirly water and is used often by beginner groups for instruction. WATCH OUT FOR JET BOATS. The section contains two rapids, Washing

Machine and Haybarn. Haybarn surfing is exemplary at around 260 cumecs. Remember that access to this area is a privilege not a right. Please leave all gates as you find them.

Since 1995 a jet boat operation has been using the river and on a busy day this boat will pass through the channel several times an hour. They have developed a signal system, described on a notice at the parking area. Keep a careful watch for it. It may be worth stopping at the registration point and letting them know you will be using the wave, especially mid week when they are not expecting people to be there.

Camping is allowed at the site; please leave it in better condition than you found it. The water from the river is undrinkable, so take your own. Boiling water kills off the water's biological elements, but leaves the naturally occurring chemical elements of arsenic and mercury intact. People have contracted the 'Fuljames Bot' from paddling there, so beware. (Fuljames was the surname of the farmer who once owned the land adjacent to the rapid. Many still use this name for the area.)

WAIKATO RIVER
HUKA FALLS

Yo—one for the picture book, especially if you get arrested. Get hard, get brave and get a full head of steam as you head down the tongue on the left side. This is the place to be.

Huka (huka = foaming or like sugar) was paddled for the first time in December 1981 by Greg Oke and Nick Kerkham. Like many of the hard case first descents in the early eighties these guys were in fibreglass slalom boats (they only used one set of gear and swapped it over after each run). By 1985 the falls had been paddled about a dozen times, once by some guy on a tube (Maybe it was Jeff—see Jeff's Joy, Rangitaiki). Things got sticky for a while through the late 1980s when a couple of people were carted off by the police. A precedent setting case was attempted by the harbourmaster and there was supposedly a fine of $10,000 for anyone caught paddling the falls. This absurdity prompted a series of editorial comments throughout the nation championing our 'right to adventure'. Since then nothing has been heard.

A video was shot in the late 1980s of some people rafting the falls at a high flow. Planned for use in an advertisement, it was never aired because some feared the impression would be given that anyone could run Huka (despite the fact the video graphically showed the raft being ripped in two and totally destroyed after recirculating into the base of the falls). Thankfully the crew were spread far and wide around the base, all in good shape.

CLASS:	IV-V+
LEVEL:	40-200 cumecs (40-90 is a good first time flow)
GAUGE:	ECNZ flow phone 0800 820 082. Listen for the flow below the Taupo control gates
LENGTH:	5km
GRADIENT:	50m/km
TIME:	1 minute
PUT IN:	above the falls on river right, or paddle down from Reid's Farm
TAKE OUT:	100m below the falls on river left
SHUTTLE:	0km
MAPS:	NZ Topo U18
CHARACTER:	big waterfall, fun gorge lead in
HOT TIP:	take a deep breath and remember that the most famous person to drown here was, after all, bound in bondage and discipline gear!!

Huka gained national notoriety in 1993 when a kayaker from Auckland died in an attempt. Since then all has been quiet on the media front, but not on the paddling scene. Plenty of people have been active. Most 'huka virgins' catch the falls at a low flow (35-80 cumecs) when the lead in is quite manageable and there is plenty of time to hit that left line at the drop. It is possible to flat land the drop and pretty much keep your face dry. Huka has been hand-paddled, double-kayaked, surfed, splatted and run several times a day. The first solo female descent was by Niki Kelly, in early 1996.

As far as the law goes I would suggest prudence in your timing—go either early morning or early evening. It is often concerned, but ill-informed members of the public who cause the most trouble, although it's less common these days.

To get to the put in: Huka Falls is on the Waikato River 4km below Taupo. Follow the signs. If you can't find it for yourself, you certainly won't find your way off the edge. Make sure to have a photographer on hand to record your efforts for the purposes of impressing your friends.

Never ever forget, kayaking is an underwater sport. Sarah Moodie evolving gills on the Wairoa. (Andi Uhl)

CHAPTER THREE

CENTRAL NORTH ISLAND

Rich in natural history, legend and beauty, cold, clear central North Island rivers flow from the high, volcanic plateau. Here the mountains of Tongariro National Park brush shoulders with the sky and gaze at their reflection in the huge drowned crater of Lake Taupo. Like their mountainous parents, the rivers here are generally placid and meek. But when rain falls the rivers come alive and the paddling is world class.

Maori gods and warriors are central to the mythology surrounding central North Island rivers. Long ago all the mountains, including Taranaki, Tauhara and Putauaki stood close together on the plateau. All were males and all were in love with the beautiful Pihanga. A terrible battle erupted amongst them. Tongariro won and Taranaki fled to the west leaving the great gash of the Wanganui River in his wake. Putauaki travelled northeast until he was halted by sunrise, with the Rangitaiki River flowing beside him. He is now more commonly known as Mt Edgecumbe. Tauhara limped away and by dawn had only reached the shores of Lake Taupo, near the white cliffs, where he remains, gazing at his lost love forever.

If gods had an impact on the landscape, modern human influence on the central plateau rivers is more obvious. In an incredible engineering feat and example of our control over nature, the 320 megawatt Tongariro hydroelectric scheme diverts rivers all round the mountains through the underground Rangipo power station, Lake Rotoaira, and into the Tokaanu power station. Massive tunnels built in the early 1960s take water from the headwaters of the Wanganui River on the western side of Mount Ruapehu, creating a 2500 square kilometre catchment for the entire scheme. The project was considered forward thinking in the 1960s and it's a shame that no-one fought to protect kayaking interests as they did for the Wairoa (see Wairoa River description). The Ruapehu eruptions of 1995 silted up the Rangipo station with enough volcanic ash to close it down for several months, giving paddlers a welcome, though brief, return to past flows on the Tongariro River.

The plateau around the Tongariro National Park offers a range of day trips. Many depend on a good dousing of rain, but with an average annual rainfall of 3600mm this is normally no problem. Weather here is dictated by the volcanoes. Warm moist air from the Tasman Sea is lifted over the mountains and falls as rain. Floods are common, and double the flow in most rivers doesn't present immediate dangers. 'Normal' flows these days are far less than natural flows before the water was diverted for electricity production. Midsummer temperatures can be very hot (25-30 degrees C) and much of the boating dries up completely.

The rivers of the central plateau are entrenched in relatively recent volcanic deposits. Rivers have carved out steep sided gorges through layers of soft ash and tephra. Ash layers from successive eruptive events are easily identified by their different colourings. Keep an eye out for rocks containing sea shells—evidence that the area was once a shallow water marine environment.

One of the most violent and devastating eruptions ever recorded occurred around AD 186 from a caldera now occupied by the waters of Lake Taupo. Up to 100,000 cubic kilometres of volcanic debris was spewed out, reaching 50km into the air (dust from this eruption was recorded in the Northern Hemisphere). Hot material blown out sideways from the vent flattened and carbonised forests, the remains of which can be seen as charcoal buried in deep layers of pumice. Silver and red beech forests at higher altitudes before the eruption were mostly replaced by podocarp forests which are able to recolonise faster than beeches. Small pockets of beech seen today probably originated from a few survivors of the blast tucked away in sheltered sites.

If you have 'ticked' all the published runs in the region then try some of the other secrets. The upper section of the Tongariro from Waipakihi is a great II+ to III section, when there is enough water. The Whangaehu River provides an interesting outing (this is the very acidic river that drains the crater lake of Mt Ruapehu) with some solid class III water. The Makatote and Mangaturuturu on the western side of the mountain reveal hidden gems when it's raining. If you want some real adventure try the Poutu Stream from the Rotoaira intake to SH1—take an abseil rope!

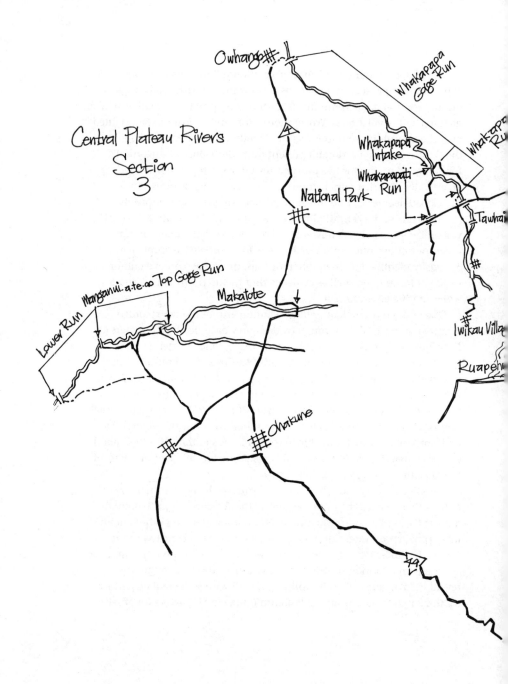

Central Plateau Rivers
Section
3

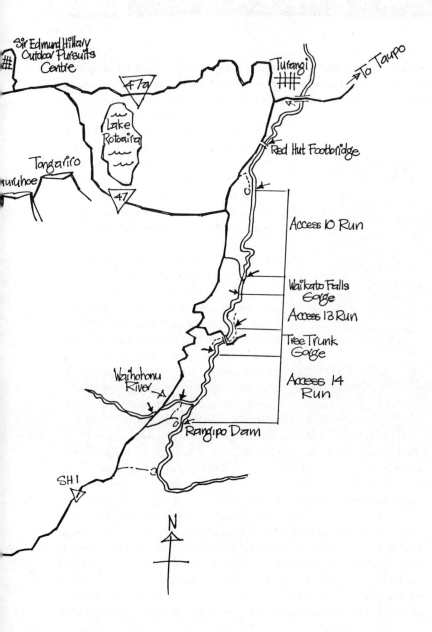

WHAKAPAPANUI

Two rivers combine to make the Whakapapa River—the Whakapapaiti and the Whakapapanui. Of these, the Whakapapanui is the easier, more spectacular and scenic of the two. Like most Central North Island rivers they are rain dependent because of their small catchment area. Below 20 cumecs the rivers are very scratchy. But don't be put off. This area offers world class boating when rain is falling, and believe me it falls a lot. Above 50 cumecs be prepared for a no-holds-barred rollercoaster with few places to decide that you don't want to be there!

On the Whakapapanui the rapids come in quick succession and boat scouting is the only feasible method of inspection. Most require boulder dodging to get the right line to avoid the inevitable wall at the bottom. What you find at the start of the run is indicative of everything down to the confluence with the Whakapapaiti. If disaster strikes in the first few rapids, gullies provide ways to escape up onto farmland on the right side of the river.

CLASS:	III-IV
LEVEL:	20-50 cumecs
GAUGE:	ECNZ flow phone 0800 820 082
LENGTH:	6km
GRADIENT:	18m/km
TIME:	1-2 hours
PUT IN:	below Matariki Falls
TAKE OUT:	Whakapapa Dam
SHUTTLE:	10km
MAPS:	NZ Topo S19
CHARACTER:	small water, technical gorge, stunning scenery and location
HOT TIP:	a little ripper, watch for whio (blue ducks)

At the confluence the river becomes wider with bigger, and at times, challenging hydraulics. One large square rock forms a particularly weir-like hole in which some have spent a good deal of penalty time.

Once at the dam, take out on the left and carry around it. Put in again and ferry across to the carpark.

To get to the put in: find the Whakapapanui river on SH47 (about 5-6km from the junction with SH48. Park about 600m west of the actual road bridge by a fence and gate. Go through the gate and aim about two o'clock. Walk 700m across the paddock to the boundary fence and look for the track heading into the bush down to the river. Beware—this steep, muddy track is probably the most dangerous part of the trip. There are numerous stories of people slipping, letting go of their boats and watching them careen down the track, around seemingly impossible corners, and launching into the river to be found later in the day. At least you'll have someone to drive shuttle.

To get to the take out: from the put in drive east on SH47 for 6km to the signposted turnoff to Whakapapa Intake. Follow this road to its end at the dam.

At around 50 cumecs you can put in to the Whakapapanui at the bridge at the uphill end of Whakapapa Village. This gives a very fast and tight run with high objective danger from logs. I looked at this for years driving up to the skifield. In 1994 Paul Chaplow and I put in after the flow had peaked and made it most of the way to Tawhai Falls before Paul had a swim after being pinned. The resulting gear chase found only the boat. From here we opted for a botanical study and headed across country to the road through very dense bush (how does 800m in 1¼ hours sound?). This section comes at you very fast with virtually no chance to scout. It is a class V- run mainly because of the speed of the water and the number of river-wide trees which must be portaged. Tawhai Falls is paddleable. Richard Sage has continued on to the SH47 road bridge. Richard highly recommends the paddle down to the top of the standard put in. This involves class III+ rapids below the SH47 bridge, a 3m waterfall, then the arrival at the top of Matariki Falls. He suggests throwing your boat off the falls then jumping in after it! You decide.

Kayaking can be a team sport. (Ian Trafford)

WHAKAPAPAITI

Yahoo—it's raining hard and has been for a few days. Get on the phone and check the flow. If the flow into the Whakapapa tunnel is more than 40 cumecs drop everything and get to the river.

CLASS:	IV V
LEVEL:	class IV: 20-50 cumecs class V: >50 cumecs
GAUGE:	ECNZ flow phone 0800 820 082. Flow into the Whakapapa tunnel, then take about 40%
LENGTH:	9km
GRADIENT:	20m/km
TIME:	1-2 hours
PUT IN:	Road bridge on SH47
TAKE OUT:	Whakapapa Dam
SHUTTLE:	16km
MAPS:	NZ Topo S19
CHARACTER:	fast, even gradient, small, technical riverbed
HOT TIP:	watch out for fencing wire across the river

From the SH47 bridge, there isn't a lot of time to think about much except how cold it is in the water, and how warm it was in the car. The water is continuous class IV, even-gradient rapids all the way to the confluence with the Whakapapanui. From here to the dam is much bigger, but less technical.

The Whakapapaiti is a faster, more technical run than its eastern cousin, the Whakapapanui. Speed, and the river's continuous difficulties, combine to add an extra point to the classification, hence class IV. At some points channel decisions have to made—and quickly. Once at the confluence with the Whakapapanui the speed eases but the volume increases, as does the size of the hydraulics. Have fun.

Whatever the flow at the Whakapapa Dam, the Whakapapaiti will have 40% of it—for example, if there is 50 cumecs at the dam, the Whakapapaiti will have roughly 20 cumecs. So it needs slightly higher flows to make it worthwhile.

To get to the put in: find the Whakapapaiti bridge on SH47 just west of the SH48 turnoff to the Chateau. Scramble down the bank to the river. There is a parking area on the river left side of the bridge if you are leaving a vehicle.

To get to the take out: head east on SH47 for about 8km, look for a sign to Whakapapa Intake. Follow this road 8km to its end at the dam.

WHAKAPAPA RIVER

The Whakapapa, like many of the rivers stretching out from the Central Plateau, is a hidden treasure. Many boaters don't know of its existence, let alone the quality of the paddling to be had. Unfortunately you'll have to wait until it has rained hard for a couple of days before it can be run.

The Whakapapa intake is the first in a line of intake structures known as the western diversion. These structures take the water from the rivers and send it via a big tunnel to Lake Otamangakau and subsequently on to Lake Rotoaira on the northern end of Tongariro National Park. The water is then piped underneath Mt Tihia and down to the Tokaanu Power Station.

When the rain falls hard enough the tunnel can't cope with the water so it's released into its natural river bed—that's what we want. Once in the river the world as you know it is quickly left behind as you are swept around the first of many corners, beyond the reach of any vehicle support. Many rapids are in the class III+ range, and these will keep you more than occupied. If you're taking a break, check out the spectacular stands of rimu forest, and keep an eye, or ear, out for the shy whio (blue duck). The very last rapid underneath the Owhango bridge is quite steep and often half a grade harder than most other rapids on the river.

CLASS:	III-IV IV-V
LEVEL:	class III-IV: 25-60 cumecs class IV-V: >60 cumecs
GAUGE:	ECNZ flow phone 0800 820 082, flow below Whakapapa Dam
LENGTH:	23km
GRADIENT:	14m/km
TIME:	4-6 hours
PUT IN:	Whakapapa Dam
TAKE OUT:	Whakapapa bridge at Owhango
SHUTTLE:	40km
MAPS:	NZ Topo S19
CHARACTER:	wilderness, scenic, even gradient bouldery riverbed
HOT TIP:	no kayaking CV is complete without this one

Floods occur regularly on central plateau rivers and can get quite big. The Whakapapa turns into a raging monster (which is great fun!) at around 100 cumecs and can rise with startling speed (150 cumecs plus in two hours). Take this into account when choosing a team for a high water run because it's difficult to escape the riverbed if anyone becomes separated from their gear.

To get to the put in: the road to the put in is signposted Whakapapa

Intake and is off SH47, 7kms east of the SH47/SH48 turnoff to the Chateau. Follow the road to its end at the Whakapapa dam.

To get to the take out: find the small settlement of Owhango on SH4 between National Park and Taumarunui. Turn off at Owhango at the sign to the Whakapapa River. Drive 2.3km on a gravel road down to the bridge.

The Butt Naked Canoe Club enjoys its annual outing on the sunny Mohaka. (Paul Chaplow)

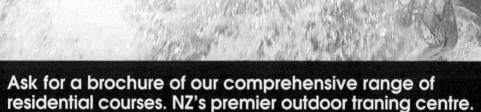

MANGANUI-A-TE-AO
RIVER: TOP GORGE RUN

The Manganui-a-te-ao ('the great stream of the land') has the dubious distinction of being the only remaining central plateau river that's not been diverted into the Rangipo Hydro Scheme. It is important that it stays this way.

CLASS:	III+ to IV-
LEVEL:	any, but high flow is best
GAUGE:	gauge at Ruatiti Domain
LENGTH:	8.5km
GRADIENT:	11.5m/km
TIME:	2-3 hours
PUT IN:	Hoihenga Bridge
TAKE OUT:	Ruatiti Domain
SHUTTLE:	9.5km
MAPS:	NZ Topo T20
CHARACTER:	single braid, pool-rapid-pool gorges, very scenic
HOT TIP:	watch for whio (blue ducks) and try not to disturb them

The river, like its many tributaries, has cut a very deep path through the ash layers that make up the local terra firma. These deep slot gorges provided railway builders with plenty of headaches by forcing the construction of large viaducts across their depths. Other streams in the vicinity offer interesting paddling in high flows. Of note is the Makatote which has a stunning class III+ run from the viaduct down to the Manganui-a-te-ao.

The highest put in on the Manganui-a-te-ao is the old Hoihenga Bridge. A track on river right leads down to a small beach. Once you push off you are into what is known, awesomely, as the Top Gorge. This is the crux of the Manganui experience and is excellent in flood levels. The rapids are a series of large waves and hydraulics. Now and then they crash into a wall at the bottom, but there is usually a good pool at the bottom of each rapid. At very high flood levels the rapids reach class IV.

Below Myers bridge (a small footbridge which can be reached on the river right side if someone needs to leave the river) the river widens and the rapids ease to fun class II-III down to the bridge at Ruatiti Domain. A slalom race is held each year on the rapid at the domain. Between Ruatiti and the bridge at Makakahi is mostly class II water with some long flat stretches. If you miss the bridge at Makakahi then you are stuck with the trip all the way down to the next road access at Pipiriki on the Wanganui River.

To get to the put in: turn west off SH4 about 4km north of Raetihi township and follow signs to Ruatiti. At a road junction near the Orautoha school, the road splits and becomes Pukekaha Rd and Ohura Rd. Follow Pukekaha Rd for about 3.5km to a fork. Take the left fork to the Hoihenga bridge. The last 100m down to the bridge is steep and slippery, so your average car is best left at the top of the final zigzag.

To get to the take out: go back to Orautoha school. Follow Ohura Rd for just over 4km to the bridge at the Ruatiti Domain.

Classic Kiwi Shuttles #1. (Graham Charles)

WAIHOHONU RIVER

The Waihohonu, which literally means 'deep water', is a small creek born from a spring on the eastern side of Mt Ngauruhoe. It flows east under SH1 to a hydro intake immediately above its meeting with a pubescent Tongariro River.

CLASS:	III
LEVEL:	15-30 cumecs
GAUGE:	Tokaanu Power Station 07 386 1210, flow at Waihohonu Intake
LENGTH:	3.5km
GRADIENT:	16m/km
TIME:	1-2 hours
PUT IN:	Waihohonu Road Bridge off SH1
TAKE OUT:	Waihohonu intake structure
SHUTTLE:	5km
MAPS:	NZ Topo T20
CHARACTER:	scenic, moderate creek boating
HOT TIP:	portage on the left side. You'll see what I mean

Most kayaking trips start their journey off SH1. It is possible to walk up the Waihohonu track for 15 minutes and put in on the Ohinepunga stream that winds across to join the Waihohonu immediately above the road bridge. While most of this upper stretch involves riding a hydroslide of water with overhanging bush, there are two drops that require more skill than simply keeping your kayak pointing downstream. Both drops are runnable, but the lack of eddies and the twisting nature of this section makes for some 'interesting' boating. A two-tiered drop (viewed from the SH1 bridge) announces your arrival at the Waihohonu proper. This last drop requires a streamlined paddle orientation, unless grappling your blade from the flora as you hand brace over waterfalls is your preferred style.

From the main road bridge the intensity eases for a couple of fun class II kilometres, then picks again up when the river steepens and converges into a short chasm. This entry rapid is worth scouting as the water funnels into a gorge 265cms wide. The precise width is all part of useless paddling trivia you glean from seeing an Acrobat 270 wedged across the gorge. Fortunately the paddler exited before the boat flexed and released from this entertaining alignment. A second rapid follows that sports a mean hydraulic at its base. It has only seen a couple of somewhat unplanned runs to date. A tightly-timed rescue of a swimmer immediately above this rapid left James Griffin little choice but to turn, paddle with adrenalin-fuelled muscles, and clear the hole away from the abandoned boat, which was pulling rodeo moves within. Portaging river left offers the easiest line. Once back in the water the river eases off for the final scenic kilometre to the intake structure and the take out on river right.

To get to the put in: once on SH1, 31km south of Turangi, the Desert Rd crosses the Waihohonu River. Put in from the southern side of the bridge. For the upper section continue south along the Desert Rd for 800m. The start of the Waihohonu track is signposted on the right.

To get to the take out: head south on SH1 for 700m. Take the first turn on the left marked Kaimanawa Forest Park, Rangipo Intake. Drive down this road for about 3km and look for a gravel road on the left. Follow this for 600m to the intake structure.

Linda Wensley

When water gets in your eyes what do you wash it out with?? Donald Johnstone finds out in Dent Falls, Arahura River. (Graham Charles)

TONGARIRO RIVER
ACCESS 14 RUN

When the rain falls hard enough, the upper reaches of the Tongariro River start to flow. When this happens, pay a visit. The highest commonly-run section is from Rangipo Dam to the top of Tree Trunk Gorge. This is Access 14, the number of the hydro road servicing the dam.

CLASS:	III-IV
LEVEL:	20-50 cumecs
GAUGE:	ECNZ flow phone 0800 820 082, flow below the Rangipo Dam
LENGTH:	6km
GRADIENT:	16.5m/km
TIME:	1-3 hours
PUT IN:	below the Rangipo Dam
TAKE OUT:	river left side above Tree Trunk Gorge Bridge
SHUTTLE:	18.5km
MAPS:	NZ Topo T19, T20
CHARACTER:	even-gradient rapids, plenty of them, fantastic scenery
HOT TIP:	don't miss the take out

The run is similar to the traditional Access 10 run, but the rapids are steeper, with more technical moves. There are far too many rapids to single any out. Suffice to say the steepness and speed of the water make it slightly harder than the other runs on the Tongariro.

The most important thing to be aware of is the take out. A large round sign on river left warns of the impending take out eddy. Make 100% sure you are in it. Don't mess with this area at all. If you miss the take out eddy it's a one way trip to the big white room in the sky as Tree Trunk Gorge is just 100m downstream. To date no one has survived the wash and rinse cycle in this narrow nightmare of trees and big drops. Make the take out!

To get to the put in: drive along the Desert Rd between Waiouru and Turangi. About 33km south of Turangi look for signs to Rangipo Intake, Kaimanawa Forest Park. Drive six kilometres down this road to the dam. Put in below the structure.

To get to the take out: return to the Desert Rd and head north to the next turnoff and signs to Tree Trunk Gorge, Kaimanawa Forest Park. Drive to the bridge over Tree Trunk Gorge. A track on river left goes down to the take out eddy. If it is your first time on the run it's worth walking down to identify the eddy.

TONGARIRO RIVER
ACCESS 13 RUN

A slightly easier run than its upstream cousin—the rapids are similar in style, but the gradient and speed more gentle. The scenery is excellent, and the Pillars of Hercules add to the interest. This run has a tricky take out, and if you miss it you will be into the as-yet-unrun gorge above Waikato Falls. To avoid this unpleasant demise, keep an eye out for overhead power lines a few rapids below the Pillars. After the wires there is one more rapid. Take out in the eddy at the bottom of this rapid. You will eventually see the sign which warns of impending doom, but not until you are in the eddy and looking for it.

If you're in the area and this catchment's going off, string 10, 13 and 14 together (taking out between them of course) over a few days—it is well worthwhile.

To get to the put in: drive down the Tree Trunk Gorge Rd off SH1 (see Access 14 take out). Cross the bridge and follow the road for 300m. A gravel road heads off to the right. Immediately opposite look for a track on the left. About 50 metre's walk down the track, you will find an in-situ handline. Climb and grovel down to the river.

To get to the take out: return to SH1 and drive north until you see signs to Waikato Falls. Turn and drive about 2.5km. On the right, opposite the road down to the Poutu Intake, is a gravel road. Follow this road (staying left at any junctions) for about 600m and park. A bush track leads to the steep muddy bank (about which you'll soon be using expletives to describe!).

CLASS:	III+
LEVEL:	20-40 cumecs
GAUGE:	ECNZ flow phone 0800 820 082, flow from Rangipo Dam
LENGTH:	5km
GRADIENT:	14m/km
TIME:	1-3 hours
PUT IN:	below Tree Trunk Gorge. A walking track leads along side the river. There is a steep bank to lower boats down
TAKE OUT:	on river left side at the bottom of the first rapid after the overhead power lines
SHUTTLE:	17km
MAPS:	NZ Topo T19
CHARACTER:	even gradient, moderate rapids, spectacular scenery through the Pillars of Hercules
HOT TIP:	a rare trip but well worth it

TONGARIRO RIVER
(ACCESS 10 RUN)

The Tongariro River is named after the mountain of the same name. Tongariro means 'seized by the south wind'; when the mythical chief Ngatoro-i-rangi was on the summit of Tongariro and in danger of perishing with cold, he called to his sisters in Hawaiiki for fire with the words, "Ka riro au I te tonga", or "I am seized by the south wind".

This is a beautiful section of river with much to offer at a range of levels. Boisterous boulder riffles provide all the excitement needed for a class III trip when the water is low (15-40 cumecs). Take time to enjoy the surrounds as you crash down the 75-odd rapids in this stretch. Try not to turn over as many of the rapids are so shallow you risk hitting your head—hard.

Surfing and playing between 40-120 cumecs is excellent. The rapids don't change much, there is just a lot more water covering the rocks. Remember, if this river was flowing naturally it would run at around 40 cumecs, so it can easily take this amount without appearing to be in flood. This flow is definitely the time to catch it.

The big runs (120-400 cumecs) are interesting. The river reaches flood point around 120 cumecs. The major problem at these levels is the speed with which the river piles into many of the sharp corners. Buffer waves just keep getting bigger, easily reaching 1.2-1.6m high, accompanied by very confused water afterwards.

CLASS:	III-III+ III+ to IV- IV+
LEVEL:	class III-III+:15-50 cumecs class III+ to IV: 50-150 cumecs class IV+: 150-145 cumecs
GAUGE:	ECNZ flow phone 0800 820 082, flow below Poutu Intake
LENGTH:	12.5km
GRADIENT:	16m/km
TIME:	2.5-5 hours
PUT IN:	Rangipo Dam. Permits granting access to the put in can be obtained from the Turangi Information Centre in Turangi
TAKE OUT:	Blue Pool or Red Hut Bridge
SHUTTLE:	14km
MAPS:	NZ Topo T19
CHARACTER:	small volume, even gradient, single braid boulder channels
HOT TIP:	if it's flowing between 80-150 cumecs drop everything and get there!

In 1990 Peter Kettering, Hugh van Noorden, Garth Falloon, Mick Hopkinson and myself put in at Rangipo at 450 cumecs and rising. (It peaked at 1050 cumecs at the Turangi SH1 road bridge.) It was a HUGE run with high objective danger from the turbulence of the water and the amount of debris travelling down the river. It took just 48 minutes for the 14.5km run to Red Hut footbridge. We had to do it again to make sure it was as good as we thought, and it was! Hugh took a very bad 3km swim, bringing home the severity of paddling at these flows. Don't try it unless you are very competent and have a strong team who understand the golden rule of paddling flooded rivers—'never, ever swim'. Fortunately Hugh and his boat washed up in the same section of trees and we were able to complete the run. At levels over 150 cumecs the weir at Rangipo Dam runs. Don't even consider paddling this, it has already claimed two lives from two attempts!

To get to the take out: find the Poutu Stream bridge on SH1 about 7km from Turangi. On the southern side of the bridge is a turnoff. Drive 2.3km of gravel to the roadend and carpark at Blue Pool.

To get to the put in: return to SH1 and head south for 8.5km to a signposted turn to Waikato Falls. Follow this for 2.8km to a left turn signposted Waikato Falls/Beggs Pool. A further 450m sees you at the Rangipo Dam. Park on the river right. Burglaries are common so take your valuables with you and lock your vehicle.

CHAPTER FOUR

T A R A N A K I

Taranaki, the land of dairy farmers, is dominated by the gentle, conical symmetry of Mt Taranaki, a snow-capped volcano with forested slopes runnelled by streams and rivers radiating into the surrounding ringplain. Most of these rivers begin as small steep creeks on the mountain, then before you know it they've picked up more water and reached the flat lands, meandering down to the Tasman Sea.

Taranaki is sacred to Maori, in mythology one of the warriors banished from the central plateau by Tongariro after their fierce battle for Pihanga (see Central North Island introduction). Mt Taranaki now stands in majestic exile, an awesome sight when he shakes off his cloak of cloud. The first climb to the 2518m summit was reputed to have been made hundreds of years ago by the chief Tahurangi. German scientist and humanist, Dr Ernst Dieffenbach, and James Heberley, a whaler, climbed the peak in 1839, the first Europeans to venture onto the sacred slopes beyond the bushline.

Mt Taranaki is thought to have begun forming about 125,000 years ago, and by 35,000 years ago had reached an estimated height of 2700m. Eruptions and erosion almost halved its height until 20,000 years ago when a new cone rose above the remains of its predecessor. The last devastating eruption occurred about 1500 AD. Inland, the high country is older tertiary mudstone up to 20 million years old. Once a vast plateau sloping westward from the Tongariro mountains, erosion has created narrow steepwalled river valleys separated by flat ridges. The most famous of these valleys contains the Wanganui River.

Because most of the rivers in the region originate close to the ocean they tend to be short. They don't carry much water so most can't be paddled until rain has filled them. Normally this isn't a problem—there is a saying "If you can't see the mountain it's raining. If you can see it, it's going to rain." Mt Taranaki is a magnet for the same westerly weather patterns that produce plentiful rain on the west coast of the

South Island. Rain falls on average 166 days a year, though the climate is mild and summers receive a large dose of sunshine. As a result Taranaki is a lush, green region of rolling dairy pasture made fertile by millenniums of volcanic ash falls.

Beginners must sample the Waitara and, still in north Taranaki, try the Mokau in low flow with a few portages. The Mokau is great fun with a good amount of water, as is the Waiwhakaiho. For extra excitement, and if you've done the better known runs, head south around the coast from New Plymouth and find the Stony River. This has a steep upper section (accessible by road) that is guaranteed to keep your heart in your mouth. East of Taranaki's mudstone hill country, don't miss out on the Wanganui River from Taumarunui, which offers some of the most beautiful easy cruising in the country. It has a guidebook of its own!

Rivers of Taranaki
Section 4

MOKAU RIVER

If it rains, go there. While Mokau means 'without any' this doesn't apply to the whitewater—or brown water in this case. The Mokau is Taranaki's largest river and is worth travelling to when there's sufficient water in it. The great thing is that mid week you can call the Wairere Falls power station (07 877 8525) to find out the flow.

The top section of the river is in a greywacke bedrock gorge and contains a number of ledge type drops up to two metres high. All of these can be boat scouted in most flows and are easily portaged. Little Huka is the only named rapid, created by a dramatic narrowing of the river with a short drop. Willows make up most of the objective danger in these top rapids, especially as the river runs a murky brown colour all the time and anything below the surface is difficult to see. Easy class II and III rapids lie below Little Huka as the river quietens down for a few kilometres.

A change in rock type is obvious as you enter the limestone of the scenic Totoro Gorge. Areas like this in New Zealand are uncommon, but just as you are enjoying the view, the river drops out of sight among huge limestone boulders. This is the hardest rapid on the river. It is a technical drop in low flows, but a raging monster at high water (>200). Either run the rapid or portage on the left side being careful of tomos hidden in the grass.

CLASS:	II-IV IV
LEVEL:	class II-IV:125-215 cumecs class IV: >215 cumecs
GAUGE:	Wairere Power Station immediately downstream of the small bridge
LENGTH:	14km
GRADIENT:	6.5m/km
TIME:	3-5 hours
PUT IN:	Wairere Falls Power Station
TAKE OUT:	Mokau Bridge
SHUTTLE:	11.5km
MAPS:	NZ Topo R17
CHARACTER:	medium volume, single channel, pool-drop, lovely bottom gorge
HOT TIP:	great playing at about 225 cumec gauge

On my first trip down this stretch we were scouting the rapid and wondering if a certain hole was washing okay. We watched in macabre fascination as a bloated sheep carcass floated round the corner and dropped perfectly in the hole. Our rodeo sheep pulled a few retentive moves before continuing on in good style. We had no problems, but no-one wanted to turn over!

Flat water ensues and just below here is the Mangataoki confluence. This small tributary offers a short but fun run from the bridge on SH3 to the Totoro take out. Continuing down the Mokau, another limestone rock sieve lies around the corner, but is slightly less intense than the first one into the gorge. Below this is flat water to the road bridge.

To get to the put in: drive to Piopio on SH3 between Te Kuiti and New Plymouth. On the southern side of the road, in the middle of town is a road signposted to Aria. Follow this for about 8km to the Wairere Falls Dam on the right. Drive down the short gravel road to the power house.

To get to the take out: drive back to the sealed road and turn right towards Aria. After about 3km turn right at the T intersection onto Totoro Rd. This road turns to gravel. Stay on this road until the Mokau Bridge. It is not signposted, but is the only crossing of the river and is obvious.

If coming from the west on SH3 turn onto Totoro Rd about 3km after the small settlement of Mahoenui. This takes you directly to the take out. Continue along Totoro Rd to the put in.

Kayaking plays an active role in the devolution of the human species. (Graham Charles)

WAITARA RIVER

The Waitara, or literally 'water from a peak' is one of Taranaki's favourite novice/intermediate trips. I'm not sure how it gets this name because its headwaters are well north of the mountain.

This is a great trip for novices and the place where most Taranaki boaters get their first taste of fear and whitewater. A dozen or so bouldery rapids spread between long flat pools make up the trip. These rapids may push into class III in very high water, but generally are a comfortable home for class II boaters.

To get to the put in: immediately west of the small settlement of Waitara is Waitara Rd which joins SH3 about 15km east of New Plymouth. Follow Waitara Rd for about 8km to the junction with Everett Rd. Turn onto Everett Rd and follow this for a just over 2km. Near Rody Rd look for a large rock and a stile (steps over a fence). Park here and walk down to the river. It is necessary to phone the farmer before crossing the land.

To get to the take out: Bertrand Rd meets Waipara Rd about 3km before the Everett Rd turn off. The bridge is about 1km along Bertrand Rd. The take out is on the left side under the bridge.

CLASS:	II+
LEVEL:	optimal is 2.7m. Above 3.0m the river tends to wash out
GAUGE:	automatic voice gauge 06 752 0613
LENGTH:	10km
GRADIENT:	4m/km
TIME:	2-3 hours
PUT IN:	off Everett Rd into the Manganui. Over the stile by the big rock!! Call 06 752 0603 to ask permission to cross the land
TAKE OUT:	Bertrand Rd bridge
SHUTTLE:	7km
MAPS:	NZ Topo Q19
CHARACTER:	fun bouldery rapids
HOT TIP:	wait for the water

WAIWHAKAIHO RIVER

When the rain hits and the power station at Mangorei reports a gauge of 2.5 or more, this small river flowing off the northern slopes of Mt Taranaki turns into exciting, continuous class III+ water. As flows creep up to between 3-4, prepare for a fast moving, hard hitting, rollercoaster which is more class IV than III. The Waiwhakaiho starts off steep, high on the mountain, but the gradient falls off rapidly as the river eases out to the Tasman Sea via the northern suburbs of New Plymouth. At normal flows the river is not feasible.

From the bridge near Egmont Village down to the Meeting of the Waters, the river is steeper, faster and more technical than the lower section. The river can be run as a whole trip, or split into two sections. The lower section, from the Meeting of the Waters to Mangorei Domain, is mainly class II-III even at high flows.

The action comes very fast on the top section with one of the most testing rapids in the first kilometre. A weir and intake structure for Lake Mangamahoe requires some caution. The left bank offers the best scouting opportunities. After this, conditions ease off with a few kilometres of bouncy class II-III water down to a small gorge. Heralded by a quarry site on the right, the gorge ends in a sizeable drop to keep you on your toes then into boulder garden rapids for the last kilometre to the Meeting of the Waters.

There is a slalom site and short rapid run in the tailrace water from

CLASS:	III-IV
LEVEL:	2.0-4.0 gauge (2.5 optimal)
GAUGE:	Mangorei Power Station 06 758 9336
LENGTH:	7km to Meeting of the Waters, 7.5km to the lower bridge
GRADIENT:	Upper:14m/km, lower 8m/km
TIME:	1-2 hours
PUT IN:	SH3 road bridge 1km west of Egmont Village
TAKE OUT:	SH3 road bridge eastern side of the city of New Plymouth
SHUTTLE:	5.5km and 9km
MAPS:	NZ Topo P19
CHARACTER:	even gradient, steep continuous water in the top section
HOT TIP:	one of Taranaki's finest

the base of Taranaki Outdoor Pursuits Centre (TOPEC).

Below the Meeting of the Waters most of the difficulty lies in the style of rapids. Most have a straight upper part leading into a sharp corner where the water piles into the wall. The Slot is the crux of this section, and also where some of the best playing is.

To get to the take out: the lower take out is at the SH3 bridge over the Waiwhakaiho, on the eastern exit of the city. The Meeting of the Waters take out is off SH3 about halfway between Egmont Village and New Plymouth. It is signposted on SH3.

To get to the put in: continue south from New Plymouth on SH3 towards Egmont Village. Put in at the Waiwhakaiho Bridge just before Egmont Village.

Life's tough with good friends, good food, great rivers and stunning countryside. (Graham Charles)

CHAPTER FIVE

LOWER NORTH ISLAND

At first glance there isn't much to tempt self-respecting, adrenalin-crazed paddlers to the bottom of the North Island. But look again, especially when it's raining, and you might be surprised. Even Wellington has paddlers, which just goes to show what a hardy breed they are. They spend long periods of time praying for a storm just so they can go paddling on their local river.

Anyway it gets better as you leave the capital city and head north along the wet, western side of the Tararua Ranges—home of the Mangahao, Waiohine, and Otaki Rivers.

The Tararua Ranges, their southern extension the Rimutaka Range, and the Ruahine Ranges to the north, run up the centre of the lower North Island like a spine. The greywacke and argillite that forms the ranges are very old rocks, metamorphosed from sands and muds laid down during the Permian and Jurassic periods. They were pushed up to form the present ranges about two million years ago.

Although not high, these ranges influence much of the region's weather by trapping moist westerly winds that dump rain on the high country, leaving the east dry. The Tararua Range is frequently shrouded in cloud, rain-drenched (around 300 days a year, in fact), swept by strong northwesterlies from the sea, or coated with snow in southerly storms.

What was, in 1866, a 360ha clearing in the densely forested plains of the Manawatu, has become the home of the New Zealand canoesport industry. Palmerston North sits near the banks of the Manawatu River servicing Massey University and a huge farming district. Before the railway was built in 1876, the Manawatu River was the main transport link between Palmerston North, Foxton and the west coast. Up river, the Manawatu Gorge is used by large numbers of kayakers, in fact it's ranked as the most used section of water for recreational kayaking in New Zealand.

Although the headwaters of the Rangitikei and Ngaruroro rivers lie quite close to each other in the Kaimanawa and Kaweka ranges respectively, they flow to opposite coasts—the Rangitikei to the west and Ngaruroro to the east. The Rangitikei River's passage south, characterised by rocky gorges through the mudstone hill country west of the Ruahine Range, is one of New Zealand's classic whitewater trips. The Ngaruroro flows southeast then east before reaching the Pacific between Napier and Hastings. And despite the fact the Manawatu arises on the eastern flanks of the Ruahine, it's remarkable in that it cuts through the Manawatu Gorge and flows west to the Tasman Sea.

The Lower North is showing true potential for new runs. The Palmerston North-based 'dangerous brothers', Donald Johnstone and James Griffin have been exploring a number of hitherto unrun sections of water having decided that 6-12 cumecs of water still constitutes a kayaking trip. The Makiri gorge has yielded some interesting water and the Upper Pohangina saw its first kayak descent in May 1996. Both these runs offer good class IV-V kayaking. The Taruarau (flows into the Ngaruroro) has a good class III+, rain-dependent section, as does the Ruamahanga to the south of Carterton.

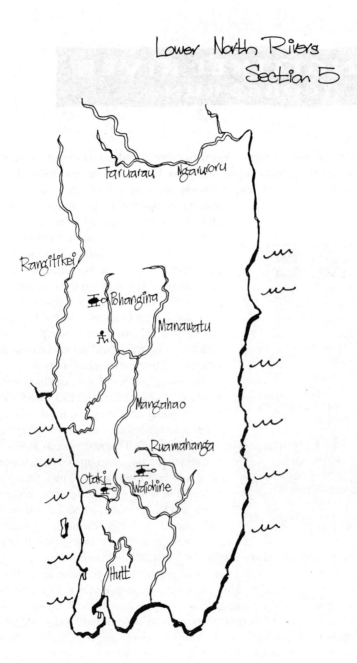

Lower North Rivers
Section 5

Taruarau   Ngaruroro

Rangitikei

Pohangina

Manawatu

Mangahao

Ruamahanga

Otaki   Waiohine

Hutt

RANGITIKEI RIVER
GORGE RUN

If there was one single river with every ingredient for the evolutionary recipe of trip into epic into story into legend, it is the Rangitikei 'day of striding out'. Take one reasonably accessible yet wild river flowing through a spectacular, deep gorge. Add several challenging drops and one extremely cool play hole. Attach a large catchment that causes the river to rise and fall dramatically in short periods of time. Put a lodge, hot showers, a big open fireplace and a bar at the take out. And if the stories don't rise to great heights on their own, add Richard Sage who works the river, has evolved his own innovative style of rock paddling, and whose unique storytelling ability has rapidly become a legend in itself.

The Rangitikei is a classic that has been paddled for years by scores of kayakers, though its early paddling history was filled with the carnage of fibreglass boats. The first explorer to the gorge was Cliff Barnett who, in 1953, attempted the run in an open canoe. It wasn't until the early 1960s that two men from Palmerston North entered the gorge again in a home-made, stainless steel canoe. It took them two seasons to get right through! The first complete kayak descent was in May 1974 by Max Grant (of 'Max's Drop'), Peter Sutcliffe and Dennis Oppatt.

CLASS:	IV IV+ to V
LEVEL:	class IV: 2-6
	class IV+ to V: 4-12
GAUGE:	River Valley Lodge, phone 06 388 1444
LENGTH:	10km
GRADIENT:	11m/km
TIME:	2-4 hours
PUT IN:	off Matawhero Road where it joins the river
TAKE OUT:	River Valley Lodge
SHUTTLE:	17.7km gravel road
MAPS:	NZ Topo U21
CHARACTER:	technical, tight bedrock gorge
HOT TIP:	big fun in flood

The first 6km on the river is an excellent class III warm up for the harder stuff to follow. Most excellent is Pop Up, a play hole guaranteed to get a cartwheel out of anyone who goes into it. The first real water is a short drop, called Stormy, which runs through a small gorge and into a wall at the bottom. This is followed by more easy water through the very obvious Narrows to the Lunch Spot, named because it is in fact a lunch spot, not a rapid.

Technical and bony in low flows, still technical but pushy in high flows, the gorge rapids proper follow in quick succession through the new Fallen Arch Rapid, Slip Rapid, Max's Drop, Dog Leg, Fulcrum, Etc, Foamy, Foo Fang Falls, See Thru, Picket, Rodeo, Rockslide, Waimarino, Cascade and Slalom Rapid to finish right outside River Valley Lodge. Of these Fulcrum and Foamy offer the crux of the paddling. Typical of the relatively soft strata in the area, 1996 saw the collapse of a large rock beside what used to be Arch Rapid. This created the tight, sticky at times, class IV+ to V drop called Fallen Arch.

If it's your first time down you'll probably want to scout some rapids as the line is not always obvious. More experienced paddlers should be able to boat scout everything. Check in with Brian and Nicola Megaw at River Valley Lodge before you go on the river. They have been running the Lodge and rafting the river since 1986 and are tuned into changes of rocks, trees and water levels in the river. This is not a good run to choose as your first class IV outing! Don't be misled by the average gradient. Most of the drop is in the last 1.5km.

Above six on the gauge the rapids become very pushy and time to correct any mistakes is reduced markedly. The river has been run at very high levels (8-12 gauge) and makes for a great expert trip.

From River Valley Lodge there is a fantastic 13km class I and II gorge trip—dozens of waterfalls, spectacular cliffs, bush and beautiful water. If anything, more scenic than the upper gorge. River Valley Lodge can provide details of the take out and shuttle (which is 45 minutes, one way).

The Megaws and Sages at River Valley Lodge are very hospitable. For a fee they offer camping, accommodation and food and will drive a shuttle if arranged in advance. This saves the hour long return trip to pick up cars when you could be sitting outside the Lodge drinking a celebratory beer or two! The road to the take out is private and there is a toll of $2/person. River Valley can provide flow and gauge information. They can be contacted on 06 388 1444.

To get to the put in from Taihape: follow the signs to River Valley along Wainui Rd and Otuarei Rd. If coming from the north drive 18.1km from the southern end of the Army Training Camp at Waiouru to a turn-off signposted to Moawhango, Napier and River Valley. Follow this sealed road for 9.5km to another junction, turn left and keep following signs 23km to Pukeokahu and River Valley. The road is sealed all the way to the start of the 4km farm road to the Lodge.

To get to the put in from the entrance of the River Valley farm road: drive 13.5km east on the gravel road to a grassy flat where the road meets the river.

Sarah Moodie

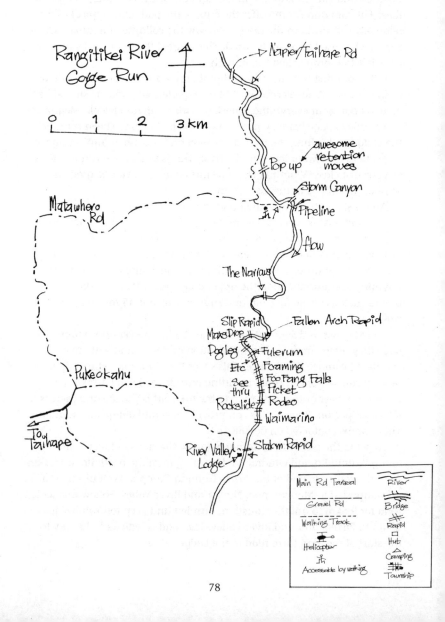

NGARURORO RIVER
LOWER GORGE

Wilderness and worth it. The Ngaruroro is a small, remote and little known river with its headwaters in the northern Kaweka Ranges. The trip is possible at any time of year, but fresh rain improves speed of travel and whitewater quality.

CLASS:	III+ to IV
LEVEL:	any, but some rain is recommended to keep the trip moving and exciting
GAUGE:	Hawkes Bay Regional Council 06 835 3164 (> 1.2 is good, 1.0 possible but very scratchy. 1.5 is high, 3 big flood)
LENGTH:	39km
GRADIENT:	7.5m/km
TIME:	4-8 hours
PUT IN:	Ngaruroro bridge at Kuripapango
TAKE OUT:	Otaumuri Stream junction, river left
SHUTTLE:	approx 55km winding gravel road
MAPS:	NZ Topo U20, U21
CHARACTER:	single channel, wild and remote gorges, scenic wilderness
HOT TIP:	very scenic trip and can be overnighted if you want. Have a staunch shuttle driver

There are a couple of trip options on the Ngaruroro. A multi-day wilderness trip can be done by flying to Boyd Hut where there is an airstrip. Most parties charter fixed wing aircraft from Taupo or Napier. From Boyd Hut to Kuripapango is class II+ and takes two to three days—a highly recommended beginner/intermediate self-support trip.

The section below Kuripapango is known as the lower gorge. With extra water it's a very long day of wilderness class III+ water. Wilderness is the operative word here and it's a great trip if you take your camping gear and stay out a night. A campsite can be found wherever you want, though the most commonly used site is halfway down the run on the left bank. (Look for a 'give way' road sign on a bluff above the river.) A manuka frame with a canvas covering, called Lindsay's Lodge, is visible from the river if you miss the sign.

From Kuripapango the water is mostly class II-III boulder gardens for the first 10km or so. The river then enters a 9km rocky gorge. This gorge contains the crux of the paddling—steep pool-drop rapids that reach class IV in high water. A narrow passage with a large rock known as The Barricade lies at the top of the last and hardest rapid. The river eases to class II as far as the Taruarau confluence and class I to the Whanawhana take out. Users beware that a southerly wind will slow you down considerably. Take extra clothing as the wind can be chilling, especially if any of your party has taken a few inadvertent dunkings.

To get to the put in: from either the Taihape or Napier/Hastings side get onto the Taihape-Napier road. It is a long drive whichever side you come in. Kuripapango is about halfway between Napier and Taihape. About 40m east of the Ngaruroro bridge is a small road which crosses a cattle grid into a Department of Conservation (DOC) rest area with an information board. Go through the gate and drive about 120m to the old DOC house. Follow the track in front of the house down to the river. Unless you have a 4WD vehicle it's best not to take the last switchback to the river.

To get to the take out: head east on the Napier-Taihape road until Otamauri. Turn right at the junction at Otamauri and follow the gravel road to the junction with Matapiro road. (The roads turns to tarseal at this junction.) Turn right onto Whanawhana Rd and drive about 1.5km to the bridge over Otamauri Stream. A track on the right side of the stream leads down to the river. It is essential that your driver goes down to the river and places some sort of marker to indicate the take out!

Indecent = if you're in up to your armpits and you don't know what's going to happen next you are 'in decent'. Pete Spiers on the Hollyford. (Graham Charles)

MANGAHAO RIVER

If you want to catch up with long lost paddling friends, just turn up at one of the spring or autumn Mangahao releases when the river becomes the busiest in the country. This is excellent for hearing the latest gossip, but removes any feeling of wilderness this run would have without all the people.

The Mangahao is dammed twice in the Tararua Ranges and its flow diverted to Arapeti Stream, then west to Mangaore Stream. The slalom site below the Mangahao Power Station makes use of this water, but use of the main Mangahao River is limited to when ECNZ release water twice a year by agreement, or when heavy rain forces them to spill water.

Having survived the very tight and winding road to the put in, a carnival scene will greet you as hundreds of kayakers, canoeists, rafters and shuttle people mill around among equipment retailers' stands and displays. Chartered helicopters fly shuttles from the take out. So much for the wilderness experience!!

Escape on to the river, which starts as a single channel in a deep bush-lined valley. A few kilometres down is the first gorge with a couple of rapids in the easy class IV range. The crux rapid in the first gorge is a series of drops through a narrow section culminating in a final rapid with some fun hydraulics. A large tree wedged at the bottom provides the objective danger in the rapid. There are some good play spots in this section, but you'll have to join the queue.

Once clear of this gorge is a long stretch of relaxing and enjoyable class II-III water. I personally enjoy getting to this section and being clear of other people on the river. The scenery is excellent.

A few harder class III+ rapids shake you out of your reverie, including

CLASS:	III-IV
LEVEL:	15-50 cumecs
GAUGE:	visual
LENGTH:	18km
GRADIENT:	9m/km
TIME:	4.5-8 hours
PUT IN:	Mangahao Reservoir No 2
TAKE OUT:	Mangahao road bridge west of Hukanui
SHUTTLE:	87km
MAPS:	NZ Topo S25, T24
CHARACTER:	single channel, small gorges, scenic
HOT TIP:	get on early, or late, to avoid the crowds

83

boulder gardens requiring active manoeuvring to stay out of trouble.
Two or three may make it to IV-, depending on the flow.

Gradually these rapids give way to easier water and the hills lay back
into pastoral land. The river becomes shallow, braided class I and II. The
take out arrives just as you decide you really didn't want a flat water
training session for the day. Often there are stalls set up selling hot dogs,
beer and other essential post-river delights. One of the tricky parts of this
run is ensuring your shuttle driver knows how to get from the put in to
the take out.

To get to the put in: go to the small town of Shannon on SH57 south
of Palmerston North. Follow signs to Mangahao Power Station. Drive
past the station up the gravel road which climbs over a saddle. It
descends slightly to Tokomaru No 3 Reservoir, skirts this and climbs
again twisting and turning like a slippery eel. Eleven kilometres from the
power station you arrive at Mangahao Reservoir No 2 and the put in.

To get to the take out: head back to Palmerston North on SH57. Find
any signs which point to Aokautere or Pahiatua Track. Follow this windy
road over the Tararua Ranges. As the road flattens onto the lowlands
near Makomako, look for a junction and right turn to Marima. Once at
Marima follow signs to Kopikopiko via Kopikopiko Rd. This road turns to
gravel a couple of kilometres out of Marima and stays this way to the
bridge. The take out is in a paddock on the river left just upstream of the
bridge. Good luck.

OTAKI RIVER
UPPER GORGE

If you are hanging around the lower North Island and you've done all the normal runs and it's raining and you're bored and you phone the Otaki River flow phone and the river's flowing around two metres on the gauge, whistle up a whirly-bird and fly up to Waitewaewae Hut in the Tararua Ranges. You won't be disappointed.

The first kilometre from Waitewaewae Hut wanders through fantastic beech forest in a small gorge. The gradient picks up and the boulder gardens start to make their presence felt. Rapids lead into each other as the gradient increases to an average of 16m/km for the first 9km of the trip. About halfway is the biggest drop in the river: Lemmings Falls, a 2.5 metre waterfall, which is worth scouting for logs. The gradient gradually relents and boulder gardens disappear, leaving you with a 3km class I/II paddle to Otaki Forks.

When the gauge reading is greater than 2m the section is probably class IV+ to V and should be treated with due respect. To date I haven't found anyone to verify this. Whatever the level, your team should be competent. It is not a great first-time class III trip because there's a long walk out if you lose your gear!

When I first did this run all the people I asked quoted times of seven to nine hours. If you are dealing with swimmers and a large team, it will take this long. We did it with a good team, in low water conditions, in four and a quarter hours.

To get to the take out: turn off SH1 200m south of the Otaki River bridge near the town of Otaki. This is signposted Otaki Gorge Rd,

CLASS:	III-IV
LEVEL:	1.5-2 lower gorge gauge
GAUGE:	flow phone 06 364 2087. Add '1' to any reading
LENGTH:	18km
GRADIENT:	11.2m/km (16m/km in first 9km)
TIME:	4-9 hours
PUT IN:	Waitewaewae Hut
TAKE OUT:	1.3km below Otaki Forks
SHUTTLE:	helicopter section 5
MAPS:	NZ Topo S26
CHARACTER:	small gorge, single channel, boulder gardens
HOT TIP:	if you really like tramping you can walk in

Tararua Outdoor Centre. After 9km the road turns to gravel for 6km to a grassy turning area and stone monument labelled Otaki Forks History. Park here and leave room for the helicopter. The track to the river is 50m back down the road. It is a good idea to go down to the river to identify the start of the track as it is well disguised. Another few kilometres along the road you'll find excellent camping if you are staying in the area.

The lower Otaki Gorge run is a very popular class I-II beginner trip. Put in on the Waiotauru near the Ranger Station a couple hundred metres above the confluence with the Otaki. Scratch and crash down to it from there. Take out (or put in for a shorter run) at Blue Slip, about 4km downriver at a swingbridge. There is a 4WD track from the main Otaki Gorge road. The next, and last, take out is at the bridge by the Tararua Outdoor Centre.

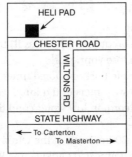

WAIOHINE RIVER

Just about everyone I spoke to about the Waiohine pronounced it differently. No wonder there was very little information about it. Wellingtonians and Wairarapa paddlers must have thought they had hundreds of rivers over their way because of this mysterious one which was something different to everyone.

"You need water, but when it's there the trip is well worth while," says Mike Savory who has probably been higher up the river than most. In the late 1980s (even Mike can't remember) a team flew to just below the forks at the top of the river. Above the forks the river was deemed too small to paddle—but who knows these days? From that point it took most of the day to paddle down to Totara Flats Hut—pleasant class III with the odd rapid that was a little harder. The helicopter can drop overnight gear off so you don't have to paddle with it—an added bonus. This leaves a few hours of class II water to the take out the next day.

The early trip was done with a river gauge reading of 1.2, which equates to about 20 cumecs. Optimal flows occur between 1.3-1.5. The Masterton Regional Council don't consider the river in flood until 2.8 on the gauge. If you are in the area and rain is falling, the Waiohine, Otaki and Hutt Gorge will all be happening as their headwaters are within a kilometre of each other.

CLASS:	III+ (IV-)
LEVEL:	1.2-2.5
GAUGE:	Wairarapa flow phone 06 379 7927
LENGTH:	18.5km
GRADIENT:	7m/km
TIME:	2 days
PUT IN:	below the top forks or at Mid Waiohine Hut
TAKE OUT:	at the road end
SHUTTLE:	helicopter section 5
MAPS:	NZ Topo S26
CHARACTER:	wilderness, scenic, fun whitewater
HOT TIP:	the river with many names

To get to the take out: from SH2 immediately north of the Waiohine River bridge a few kilometres out of Carterton turn onto Swamp Rd. Follow this for about 4km then turn right onto Moffats Rd. Two and a half kilometres along here turn left into Josephs Rd which eventually becomes Waiohine Gorge Rd. Drive to the end of the road.

HUTT GORGE

When the umbrellas are inside-out in a southerly storm, Wellington paddlers kick off their bankers' suits and race to the Hutt Gorge for a stress management session. The gorge is the most, indeed only, interesting and accessible moderate grade paddling available to Wellingtonians.

CLASS:	III-IV
LEVEL:	0.9-2 (Birchville gauge)
GAUGE:	flow phone 04 526 7264
LENGTH:	9.5km
GRADIENT:	7.5m/km
TIME:	2-3 hours
PUT IN:	Pakuratahi Forks, Kaitoke Regional Park
TAKE OUT:	next to Kaitoke Storage Lakes, Kaitoke Regional Park
SHUTTLE:	9km
MAPS:	NZ Topo S26
CHARACTER:	small gorge, single channel, short drops

Too low to paddle in normal flow, after a good southerly rainstorm it's a great trip with plenty of play spots. During a heavy rainstorm a fast class V trip is waiting if you manage to catch it. The best level (about 1.2) is above the rocky low flow and before the eddies get too boily and the play spots disappear.

The river gauge is downstream, below the confluence of the Akatarawa river. The Akatarawa tends to catch northerly rain more than the Hutt Gorge so the gauge can be misleading and needs to be interpreted with the weather patterns. When the Hutt Gorge is too high, go for an Akatarawa trip, but be careful of willows on the banks.

The first kilometre down to the pipe bridge is easier than the rest of the river. If you're not feeling confident this is the last easy take out back to the road. The first named rapid, Aqueduct, is at the end of the straight below the pipe bridge. About 2km further an overhanging cliff on the right marks Anne's Drop—a rapid worth inspecting from the left at higher flows. After Putaputaweta Stream enters on the right, the river narrows into the most difficult section—Double Drop and Corkscrew. These are difficult to inspect at high flows, but try sidling high on river right. Watch out for logs. The river eases, although there are several more rock gardens and drops before the gradient runs out and power lines above the river signal the approaching take out.

To get to the take out: about 7-8km north of Upper Hutt take the turnoff north of the Te Marua Golf Club and follow signs into the Kaitoke park. Turn left just before the pumphouse building (which contains toilets with hot air hand driers for cold southerly days) and follow the road down to the river. The gate on this road is usually locked at dusk, so don't play on the rapids too much!

To get to the put in: go back onto SH2 and drive about 8km to just south of where the road crosses the Pakuratahi river into Kaitoke Regional Park. Turn left and follow the road through camping and picnic areas to a carpark next to the confluence of the Hutt and Pakuratahi rivers. Access further up the Hutt River is restricted because the water intake provides drinking water for most of Wellington. A road continues past the ranger's residence downstream to the pipe bridge, but the gate is usually locked.

Mike Savory

And they told me kayaking would be good for my physique?? (Graham Charles)

CHAPTER SIX

NELSON/MARLBOROUGH

Sun and wine are enjoyed in equal measure by Nelson and Marlborough's kayakers. Blenheim, dubbed the Sunshine Capital, competes with Nelson for the most sunshine hours recorded in the country and both have been national winners. Nelson's other claim to fame is as the birthplace of Ernest Rutherford, the man who first split the atom. Also famous are the Marlborough Sounds, numerous national and forest parks, lakes, walking tracks, sea kayaking (uphill paddling), fertile river valleys, huge vineyards, fishing...the list goes on.

If you're passing through and haven't done any of the rivers in this chapter I can strongly recommend them. The whitewater is generally in the class II-III range, but well worth a visit. Local paddlers are very patriotic and to pooh-pooh the rivers is to ensure you will never find a shuttle driver again. At the very least take a break and partake of one of the wine trails the area is famous for.

Though Nelson and Marlborough share the same chapter they form two very distinct geographical regions separated by the Richmond Range. East of the range, extensive glaciation in the Wairau valley has left a legacy of large, gently-graded alluvial plains not entirely conducive to producing exciting whitewater. Similarly the relatively old and gently-graded nature of much of Nelson means it doesn't harbour a goldmine of whitewater runs.

Despite this Nelson has an excellent spread of rivers that, with the right amount of water, provide superb class III-IV boating. Generally, these rivers have good road access and are situated close to an excellent range of pottery shops and cafés. Whitewater worthy of note includes the Wairoa, the Motueka's play hole 'Blue Gums', and the Baton River. Other rivers worth a visit but not described here includes the Waingaro and Takaka Rivers in Golden Bay. The Roding, Maitai, Lee, Wangapeka, and Aorere also provide a range of trips and class III-IV water in floods. These rivers are generally unpaddleable at lower flows, but solid rain in

Kahurangi National Park and the Richmond Ranges can bring them up quickly.

Much of the guesswork has been taken out of striking the right water levels with the Tasman District Council's recent installation of a flow phone dispensing information on the Wairoa, Motueka, Takaka, and Buller Rivers. Readings are taken twice daily (6am and 6pm) so monitor weather conditions between these times to estimate actual flows.

Marlborough boasts plenty of easier water for novice and intermediate kayakers. While not making this book the Waihopai, Pelorus and Rai provide tens of kilometres of class I and II water. In the first three years of my kayaking career I paddled nothing else. All have quality water and offer a lot of excitement when in flood. Further south, the Clarence River, which flows from the spectacular Kaikoura Ranges, is a great multi-day kayaking journey (described on page 102).

The typical fun kayak trip

Nelson/Marlborough
Section 6

BATON RIVER

Characterised by a number of rapids through a series of rocky and picturesque gorges, the Baton River is almost a miniature version of Nelson's Wairoa River. A major tributary of the Motueka River, the Baton is a little charmer with enjoyable class III paddling and numerous play spots. It is only paddleable at higher flows after continuous northwest rain in the surrounding ranges of Kahurangi National Park. If the Motueka River at the main road bridge between Motueka and Riwaka is big and brown, flowing from bank to bank and features the occasional tree, then the Baton will probably be a happening thing. If water is flowing over the ford at the take out, then the trip's on.

To get to the put in: the notable landmark to find when going to the Baton Valley is the slightly misnamed 'Baton Bridge', which in fact crosses the Motueka River. If travelling along West Bank Rd from Riwaka, Baton Bridge is the fourth bridge over the Motueka (including the SH60 bridge). From Motueka along SH61 (the eastern bank) the Baton Bridge is the third over the river. Travel south 4km from Baton Bridge along the West Bank Rd to reach the take out immediately (we're talking metres) above the ford on river left.

To get to the put in: continue upstream 5km and put in along open river flats.

CLASS:	III
LEVEL:	high flows
GAUGE:	visual
LENGTH:	5km
GRADIENT:	9m/km
TIME:	1-2 hours (depending on flow and put in)
PUT IN:	along open river flats 5km upstream from ford
TAKE OUT:	ford 4km upstream from the Baton bridge (c. 200m upstream from confluence)
SHUTTLE:	4km
MAP:	NZ Topo M27, N27
CHARACTER:	enjoyable Class III paddling through numerous small rocky gorges. Easy access to road
HOT TIP:	catch it if you can

Sarah McRae

MOTUEKA RIVER
BLUE GUMS RAPID

Finding the surf hole Blue Gums resembles many of the answers to life's great mysteries: there are those who know, and then there are those who don't. If you lose yourself in the maze of Motueka's back roads, Hot Mama's café in Motueka is a good second option.

Blue Gum is formed by a rocky shelf located on a bend in the middle of the river. During averagely high river flows the hole consists of a small wave next to a very nice surfing hole. Generally soft and cushiony, the play hole provides good entry and exit options and an opportunity for some rollicking good rodeo practice. The continuous flat water run down the next 2-3km should satisfy even the most timid beginner 'Blue Gummer'.

Tasman District Council's flow phone measure for the Motueka River is taken at Woodstock, downstream of the confluence of the Baton. Recommended flows are 100-180 cumecs on the TDC gauge, with the optimum around 150. Above about 180 cumecs the water will be moving too fast for easy access to the hole from either eddy. Above 200 cumecs the hole will disappear.

CLASS:	II+
LEVEL:	100-180 cumecs
GAUGE:	Tasman District Council flow phone 03 544 3393
LENGTH:	20m
GRADIENT:	nil
TIME:	as much as your body can take
PUT IN:	West Bank Road NZ Topo Grid Ref N26 069 112
TAKE OUT:	see above
SHUTTLE:	nil
MAP:	NZ Topo N26
CHARACTER:	numerous
HOT TIP:	150 cumecs and the playhole is hot

To get to the put in: finding Blue Gums requires more than a basic knowledge of tree nomenclature. The small plot of alien vegetation visible from the carpark should not be relied on as a landmark. It's tempting to say 'follow your nose' from Motueka, but you'll probably end up at Hot Mamas. Blue Gums is located on the main stem of the lower Motueka River, approximately 4.5 km directly upstream from the main road bridge between Motueka and Riwaka. Ideal access is on river left. If you are driving across the bridge towards Riwaka, go straight ahead onto

Umukuri Rd at the next sharp right hand bend (less than 1 km from the bridge). Follow Umukuri Rd to the T-intersection and then turn left onto Little Sydney Rd, following the road around onto Old Mill, and then the next left onto West Bank Rd. About 1 km down this road you will first see the river, and then a gravelled left hand shoulder, with parking for about six cars. From here there's an easy put in via the five short metres of track to the river's edge.

For those trying to predict when this beast will flow, note that the Motueka River weaves an interesting east-west course through the Tasman Bay hinterlands. The headwaters of the Motueka are in the Richmond Range. The river winds westward through Kohatu, and then shifts north, with significant contributions from the Wangapeka and Baton Rivers. Heavy rain in Nelson's eastern hills will sometimes be enough to bring the river up. Watch those skies.

Sarah McRae

Classic Kiwi Shuttles #2.(Graham Charles)

WAIROA RIVER

The Wairoa River flows directly out of the rugged Mt Richmond Forest Park to emerge behind Brightwater. Within easy driving distance from nearby Nelson (30 minutes), the Wairoa provides a popular after-work run for local paddlers when the flow is right. About two days of consistent rain turns the Wairoa into a superb technical class III whitewater run with great play spots and dynamic eddy moves. Not recommended at flows less than 80 cumecs.

Access to both the take out and put in is via the Wairoa Gorge Rd on river left. Which of the four put in options you choose should depend on group experience, flow, time available, state of road and how much you prize your vehicle. The first of the put in options is at the boldly signed Wairoa Gorge Recreation Reserve, 16km from the Brightwater pub, and immediately below the confluence of the left and right branches. A further two put ins are accessed from the Old Mill Rd at the Andrews and Anslow Rd fords. These roads turn off from the Old Mill Rd at 2km (Andrews) and 4km (Anslows) above the confluence. Even higher put ins are available but note that road access above (upper) Andrews Rd ford can be marginal, particularly in wet conditions.

CLASS:	III-IV
LEVEL:	60-250 cumecs
GAUGE:	Tasman District Council flow phone 03 544 3393
LENGTH:	up to 11km
GRADIENT:	10m/km
TIME:	2.5 to 4 hours (depending on flow and put in)
PUT IN:	a number of put in sites along Wairoa Gorge roads
TAKE OUT:	take out on river right immediately before bridge at Andrews Rd, approximately 6km upstream from the Wairoa-Lee confluence (Grid Ref N28 179736)
SHUTTLE:	up to 11km
MAP:	NZ Topo N28
CHARACTER:	easy access class III rapids in rocky gorges
HOT TIP:	this river drops quickly, and there are two Andrews Roads

All options provide class III water with more technical rapids below the confluence. The choice is yours and will depend on flow and time available. The river can be scouted from many spots along the road. Trips from above the highest ford can take up to five hours.

At very high flood flows (250+ cumecs) many of the more technical rapids wash out, leaving a formidable class III+ to IV big water run with typical flood features of very fast moving current, unusual hydraulics, few eddies, and the occasional tree. We would recommend a more conservative put in below the lower ford at this flow, and overall the run should be contemplated by more experienced paddlers only. Note that at very high flood flows there are few places to inspect the harder rapids on the section below the confluence of the left and right branches and for other than experienced paddlers it is advisable to run this section only with someone familiar with the river. Any attempts to paddle the Wairoa Gorge above the weir at very high flood flows should also be approached with caution.

Flows from the TDC river gauge are taken below the Wairoa/Lee confluence. The flows given above are based on this combined flow reading.

The Wairoa Gorge is accessed from the small township of Brightwater. Head down River Terrace Rd behind the Brightwater pub, following directions to the Wairoa Gorge Rd. Access to the Wairoa's upper reaches is by continuing to follow the road up the true left bank.

When conditions are right there are a number of other trips in the area to keep you wet.

Lower Wairoa Gorge: paddlers seeking a less demanding trip can put in at the take out for the Upper Gorge section and take out directly above the weir at Max's Bush. This take out is approximately 1.5 km below the Wairoa/Lee confluence on river left. At 80-200 cumecs this section from the bridge consists of the occasional class II+ rapid.

Lee River: the Lee River is the Wairoa's main tributary and is also worth a paddle at higher flows, especially in the upper reaches. Access to the Lee is from the River Terrace Rd, turning left at the road turnoff by the Wairoa/Lee confluence to follow the Lee Valley Rd along the river's true left bank. The Lee is an easier version of the Wairoa, with similar ease of access and scouting from the road. Upper limit is at the Cement Works, where there is an access track to the river about 100m downriver from the locked gate at the end of the public road.

Sarah McRae/Geoff Miles

WAKAMARINA RIVER

The Wakamarina was the home of one of the biggest gold rushes north of the Shotover and Clutha. The story goes that in 1860 a woman washing clothes in the river one day noticed something shining on the bottom of the river. Nothing happened for a few years until the governor of the area offered a large fee to whoever could prove that the Wakamarina had gold enough for a claim. And so it began with sizeable amounts of gold extracted from the quartz veins which run through the area. The 'canvas town' near the mouth of the river was, at one stage, the largest populated area in the country.

For kayakers the river has its own golden charms. In normal flows it is a scenic cruise down some scratchy, rocky rapids with fantastic deep blue/green pools making up the in-between bits.

If you want more action in the Wakamarina wait until rain has fallen in the catchment and lifted the level. Then the rapids fill in and provide an exciting ride with plenty of moderately-sized pressure waves, hydraulics and tricky corners. The difficulties rarely push past the class III+ range.

CLASS:	II-III+
LEVEL:	1.9-3 (needs rain to get to these levels)
GAUGE:	Wakamarina bridge at Canvastown (on the bridge)
LENGTH:	7km
GRADIENT:	6m/km
TIME:	1-3 hours
PUT IN:	at the Wakamarina Valley roadend
TAKE OUT:	at the bridge by Mountain Camp Creek
SHUTTLE:	7km
MAPS:	NZ Topo O27
CHARACTER:	small volume, very scenic
HOT TIP:	allow some time to take in the history of the Canvastown Pub

To get to the take out: drive to Canvastown on SH6 between Blenheim and Nelson. Drive up the Wakamarina Valley road to Mountain Camp Creek. About 500m further on a road leads down to an old bridge. Park by this road. It is possible to paddle all the way to Canvastown or another take out at Mutton Creek.

To get to the put in: continue upvalley to the end of the road. There are a number of alternative put ins and you can access the river virtually wherever you can see it.

Great New Zealand camping sites: upper Hollyford valley, below Mt Talbot. (Graham Charles)

WAIRAU RIVER
RAINBOW RUN

As a child I watched in total horror as my father attempted to run a rapid on the lower Wairau in his newly built canvas canoe. The water was awesome (class I), the danger extreme (nil), and excitement intense (true). Needless to say he tipped out and the boat disintegrated around a rock, which only added to my already overloaded sense of awe about this weird sport.

CLASS:	II-III+
LEVEL:	anything up to huge flood
GAUGE:	visual
LENGTH:	10km
GRADIENT:	10m/km
TIME:	2-4 hours
PUT IN:	Schroders Creek near the Old Rainbow Homestead
TAKE OUT:	Rainbow Valley Skifield turnoff
SHUTTLE:	9.5km
MAPS:	NZ Topo N29, N30
CHARACTER:	single braid, interspersed boulder gardens with straight shot rapids
HOT TIP:	something different

Different sections of the Wairau River in Marlborough have been used for years by kayakers. The lower reaches below Renwick are good first timer territory and many of Blenheim's kayakers get their first taste of true fear and moving water on this stretch.

Blenheim multisport paddlers use the section from the Wash bridge down to Renwick as a good 60km braided brain number prior to embarking on the Coast to Coast multisport race. Surgeon General's warning: this sort of behaviour kills more brain cells than any sort of drug.

For true whitewater action, paddlers drive to the head of the valley for a choice of runs. The most popular is the Rainbow Run. Warm up on the first few kilometres of class II before the action picks up and the river takes on a boulder garden appearance. The main water of note on this section is the Hamilton Rapids. This is a 100m section where the gradient steepens and the boulders are big enough to create a series of drops that push the top end of class III. In higher flows this rapid may reach class IV. The rapid has an ideal scouting/watching area from a swingbridge across the river in the middle of the rapid. The rapids begin just above where the Hamilton and Lees creeks flow into the Wairau.

Below here the river eases off to the odd class II+ chutes that maintain interest on the way down to the Rainbow take out.

For those wanting a little more, drive higher up the valley to above Hells Gate. Put in near Coldwater Creek for a 3km section of steep, technical class III that pushes class IV in high flows. Below this section the river is flat and braided down to Schroders Creek.

To get to the take out: turn off SH63, between Blenheim and St Arnaud, at the signs to Rainbow Valley Ski Area. This turnoff is about 12km east of St Arnaud. Drive on this gravel road to the skifield turnoff.

To get to the put in: continue up the valley for a little under 10km to the Old Rainbow Homestead. Not far beyond the skifield turnoff is a locked gate. Phone 03 521 1838 and arrange to collect the key and pay the key deposit (some of which is refunded on return of the key.)

This is fun—and you're having it! (Ian Trafford)

CLARENCE RIVER

The Clarence River is one of the country's longest rivers, paddleable for most of its length. It is born on the eastern slopes of the magnificent Spenser Mountains. It flows south from Lake Tennyson, but swings northeast to where it has carved a route between the Inland and Seaward Kaikoura ranges. Once through these it sniffs the sea and heads sharply back southeast to emerge on the coast north of Kaikoura. Throughout almost its entire length the countryside is a stark mix of tussock high country and cleared land. Winter temperatures are bitterly cold, while in midsummer the area bakes. Spring provides optimal conditions for a leisurely end of year float down the Clarence.

The first complete descent of the river was by raft in the early 1960s. Since then the Clarence has been descended by almost every means available. Through the 1970s it was considered a challenging river run, and many canoe clubs held an annual outing to it. Times have changed and it now seems more popular as a social river expedition, with most parties using a variety of craft from kayaks, canoes and rafts to provide interest en route to the sea. The use of rafts to carry all camping equipment, and beer, seems to be the norm these days. This also opens up the experience to many who have never been on whitewater. In the era of plastic downriver racers it won't be long before people do the trip in one day.

Most whitewater action lies in the gorges where severely shattered and twisted greywacke rock provides excellent edges to rip rafts, kayaks and anything else that might run into them! The Top Gorge and the Saw Tooth Gorge rapids are in the class III range, requiring manoeuvring

CLASS:	II-III
LEVEL:	anything up to flood
GAUGE:	visual
LENGTH:	204km
GRADIENT:	3m/km
TIME:	3-4 days
PUT IN:	Acheron Bridge near the Acheron Accommodation House
TAKE OUT:	Clarence River Bridge, SH1
SHUTTLE:	175km (via most direct route)
MAPS:	NZ Topo N31, O31, O30, P30
CHARACTER:	wilderness, scenic, high country, easy multi-day trip

amongst boulder gardens to avoid the inevitable wall at the bottom.

The river can be split into three distinct sections. The logistics and campsites are yours to choose depending on how many days you are on the river.

Upper Clarence Gorge

This section extends 50km to below Palmer Stream and contains one gorge. The only rapid of note is The Chute which is a straight run over a drop into a pool. This drop is heralded by a hard bend to the left and a huge flat rock in mid stream. Most of the water in this section is shallow shoal rapids with pools in between. Once clear of the gorge the river opens out and is flanked by tussock-covered hill country.

Middle Clarence Valley and Gorge

This 70km mid section has no major whitewater, but plenty of class II boulder gardens to keep interest up. From the Gloster River confluence the Clarence flows into a deep gorge before Quail Flat and the middle Clarence valley. This easy section is overlooked by the magnificent peaks of the Inland Kaikoura Range—Mounts Alarm, Tapuae-o-Uenuku, and Mitre. The old Quail Flat and Bluff Station homesteads are also of note.

Lower Clarence Gorge

From Ravine Hut the valley narrows as the lower, or Saw Tooth Gorge approaches. This 84km section contains the most interesting whitewater of the journey. The walls of the Sawtooth Gorge are high and badly eroded, providing the material that produces the rapids. The whitewater is moderate until just downstream of Jam Stream where the Jaw Breaker lives. I can only assume the early river pioneers took some hefty physical abuse through this section as the next rapid is known as Nose Breaker. Scenic pools and flat stretches lie in between the rapids. Nearly all the rapids in this gorge are similar, with a straight rock garden line that slams into a wall at the bottom.

Placid, deep water flowing between vegetated hillsides provides a stark contrast to the open eroded country upriver. Once clear of the gorge the river braids. Choose carefully to avoid running aground in the wrong channel. The Glen Alton bridge arrives as you are becoming tired of the braids. Depending on time and conditions take out here or continue to the main road bridge. The last section has some delightful shingle chute rapids with sizeable pressure waves making an exciting end to the journey. The take out is on the true right at the bridge. Watch out for the large concrete blocks in the river around the bridge which have metal protruding in places.

Camp anywhere you want to—this is New Zealand after all! If you are using raft support go for a comfy trip and ensure you are self-sufficient for shelter. Take a map and compass, plenty of warm clothes and a good stash of beer and wine. Most parties spread the trip over three and a half days and aim for these sort of places:

Day 1 (afternoon) Acheron Bridge-Below Tinline Creek.

Day 2 Below Tinline Creek-Quail Flat

Day 3 Quail Flat-Ravine Hut

Day 4 Ravine Hut-Main Road

There are a number of musterers' huts spread down the river, but they are locked so parties must rely on their own shelter.

The lower valley is prone to strong nor'west winds and some parties, especially rafts, have been unable to make progress down the river. The best plan in these circumstances is to wait it out. Make sure everything is tied down and all river craft are weighted with large boulders. UFO sightings on the Kaikoura Coast in the 1970s were probably flying rafts belonging to unfortunate teams that didn't take these precautions.

To get to the put in from Hanmer Springs: follow Jacks Pass Rd out of the township. When the road first hits the Clarence River turn right and follow the river to the bridge at the Acheron Accommodation House along 20km of gravel road. Put in below the bridge. Before you take off make doubly sure that your shuttle driver knows the **date** and **place** to pick you up.

To get to the take out: this is on SH1 about 42km north of Kaikoura. If you want to take out, or just sightsee up to Glen Alton bridge, drive over the Clarence River bridge and turn up-valley on the first road. Follow your nose and signs to Glen Alton.

Surf Sports

Piha
Raglan
Mt Maunganui
New Plymouth
Gisborne
Waimarama
Nelson
Riversdale
Fox River
Nile River
Wellington
Whites Bay
Hokitika
Kaikoura
Sumner/Taylors Mistake
Dunedin
St Kilda

Done all the local rivers? Bored? Then try out these surfing locations.

CHAPTER SEVEN

BULLER/WEST COAST

Big rivers, small rivers, steep creeks, scenic wonderlands, multi-day trips, beginner trips, 'hair boatin' trips... you name it and the Buller/West Coast region has them all, including the unceasing attentions of millions of sandflies. The area deserves a guidebook of its own.

The kayaking landscape here owes much to the fact the region sits astride the New Zealand Alpine Fault—the collision zone between the Pacific and Indo-Australian tectonic plates which has raised the Southern Alps with incredible steepness from the West Coast. To reach the sea West Coast rivers have carved through an abrupt mountain wall of granite and schist. Characteristically the rivers are short, steep and wend their way through stunning granite or schist gorges before spilling out onto the coastal plains. Climate is the other factor that influences Buller/West Coast kayaking. As moist westerly airstreams hit the Southern Alps, rain is released in large quantities west of the Alps. Despite recording more sunshine hours than Southland or coastal Otago, rain is often very heavy—more than 25mm an hour is common. You could spend a week paddling the normal runs in glorious sunshine—and then it rains, the rivers rise dramatically, change character and have to be done again. If the weather is westerly and the barometer low, paddling the small local creeks is a good idea. Once placid little boulder gardens become serious, and the main rivers become outrageous. This is a blessing, but beware of going anywhere without knowing what to expect from the weather. Clearings come with a southerly change as the next high pressure system moves onto the country. This is the best time to hit most of the rivers, as they are dropping and when the forecast is stable for a few days.

The Buller is simply the greatest kayaking river in the country. It isn't the hardest, the longest or the biggest, but the surrounding region has the highest concentration of runs for all levels. A fact not so readily appreciated is that the Buller is the last big, natural-flowing river system in the country, draining most of Nelson Lakes National Park, and picking up the Kawatiri, Gowan, Mangles, Matiri, Matakitaki and Maruia along with a host of smaller catchments. First to canoe on the Buller were the early Maori who paddled the lower reaches well before any European presence. They were great respecters of the river's moods and power as they moved through the area on foot, seeking the highly valued pounamu (greenstone). Thomas Brunner's 1846 expedition into the Buller (or Kawatiri) Gorge was one of the epics of early European exploration in New Zealand, a 14 week marathon of starvation, and a constant battle to survive.

With so many tributaries the 'well connected' Buller has been described as the most aristocratic of New Zealand rivers. This is also why the Buller's big flows are the highest in the country (highest recorded flood level: 10,500 cumecs) and why floods happen fast. In 1989 I witnessed the Buller rise 12m overnight at the Mangles confluence. The same flood damaged the swingbridge below Ariki Falls, some 50m above mean water level. The paddling was outrageous! Along with floods, earthquakes have also shaped the kayaking scene here—the Karamea, Mokihinui, Matakitaki and Buller all feature large lakes dammed by huge landslides loosed during earthquakes. Many rapids have been caused by smaller landslides: O'Sullivans, Ariki and Earthquake Rapids on the Buller are all a result of the 1929 shake which rocked the Murchison area. Scars from when whole hillsides slid into valley floors can still be seen.

The hydro potential of the Buller system hasn't gone unnoticed by power generators who have plans for a number of hydro schemes. The worst is to build a dam near Granity Creek and flood the whole of the Gowan Valley and the Buller's upper reaches. The Buller national water conservation order, granted in 1996, protected almost all of the Buller catchment except for sections of the Matiri and Matakitaki Rivers, which were excluded. It also set minimum flow levels for the Gowan which severely restricts the scale of possible hydro development at present. As a concerned user group we must never allow any hydro scheme that will spoil this pristine river system.

Although West Coast kayaking blossomed much later than on the Buller, there is no doubt the rivers here are world class in every possible definition. They are challenging, remote, uncrowded, scenic beyond belief, and most importantly, ours to protect. Many sections of rivers were tubed or pack-floated by hunters and trampers in the 1950s and

60s. Recreational river use began in earnest using aircraft to get into the remote Landsborough and Karamea catchments sometime in the 1960s. A Whitcombe trip filmed on 35mm home movie in 1980 heightened interest in the potential of the West Coast. During the 1980s plastic boats and the desire to explore saw a number of new rivers paddled using helicopters for access. Enter Bruce Barnes in the early 1990s. Bruce is a modern day Thomas Brunner with a unique mix of toughness, a keen desire to explore and a high level of kayaking skill. He's been the real pioneer of Coast paddling and participated in most first descents of rivers and creeks in this section. Living in Hokitika with the Westland rivers on his doorstep, with his trusty dog Eddy he has walked, bashed and fought into the tops of many seemingly impossible gorges to see what lurked within. He is a mine of information and to date the only information source for kayakers venturing to the Coast for their first experience.

So, you are new to the Coast? For a moderate multi-day adventure try the Karamea, Landsborough or Waiototo. For challenge don't miss the Arahura, Perth, Whataroa, Whitcombe, Kakapotahi, Crooked and Turnbull. If it's all new, start with the Mokihinui, Hokitika, Toaroha and lower Wanganui or lower Whataroa. Masochists try the Fox and the Waiho! And for breathtaking scenery take your camera to the Kakapotahi, Crooked, Oparara and Perth. If you're in the Hokitika region and the main rivers are flooded scratch around for information on 10 Mile Creek (just north of Greymouth), try the Totara, Kaniere, Blue Bottle or Mackay creeks from your Lake Mahinapua basecamp. And if you are further south, catch Tartare Creek behind the township of Franz Josef. Be warned all of these trips will push well into class IV-V when there is water. And there's more. The Gowan River (draining Lake Rotoroa) isn't in this guide but may interest you (watch out for willows if you do it).

Of the future... new runs are being opened up as you read. The Coast has much potential yet. All it takes is a good imagination, a map, and some people to drag with you. I could list all the as yet unrun stretches that I know of, but that would make it too easy and take away one very important part of the process. Find your own and dare to adventure!

Buller Westland
Section 7A

Oparara
Karamea
Mokihinui
Buller
Murchison
Mangles
Matakitaki
Westport
Buller
Maruia
Glenroy

OPARARA RIVER

Stories about hideous class V rapids with even more hideous class VI and VII portages circulated long before the Oparara Gorge run became established—tales of boats used as bridges to cross limestone fissures and throw bags made into ladders to retrieve paddles down sinkholes.

CLASS:	IV-V (P)
LEVEL:	see description
GAUGE:	bridge pile on the right at put in
LENGTH:	12km
GRADIENT:	12m/km to Fenian Creek, 28m/km Fenian Creek to take out
TIME:	4.5-8 hours
PUT IN:	top bridge over the Oparara River
TAKE OUT:	past the quarry site 4km up Oparara Rd
SHUTTLE:	24km (16km rough gravel road)
MAPS:	NZ Topo L27
CHARACTER:	weird but interesting, there is nothing else like it
HOT TIP:	this is adventure kayaking defined

Darkness was the usual time parties emerged with wide eyes and damaged egos. The only constant was the quality of showers, coffee, beer and food at the Last Resort in Karamea.

Most of these epics were due to lack of knowledge about the flows required to descend this seemingly innocent little stream. The Oparara is adventure kayaking regardless of the flow. Be prepared for log jams, grovelling through limestone sieves, slippery portages, long stretches of flat water, no easy escape and a four hour trip at least. These are essential ingredients for the adventure aficionado and are, in a strange way, redeeming qualities. If you fail to see these as qualities, the overhanging limestone caverns and arches, rainforest, the strange tea coloured water with weird rune-like foam patterns and the whitewater are superb as an end in themselves.

Ben Willems, Sooty Love and Keith Maxstone made the first descent of the Oparara in March 1993 in a standard summer flow. They reported a scratchy, but interesting trip, taking two days to complete the journey in bath bats! Other parties established the flow parameters through the 1995 and 1996 seasons. The river needs rain, but like many things in life, moderation is the key. At the top bridge over the Oparara look under the bridge on river right. If water is lapping at the bottom edge of the concrete footing this is about optimal flow. The tolerance seems to be about 25cm higher than this or 15cm lower. Any higher or lower and you are asking for more tramping than you figure.

The first half hour on the water to Moria Arch is class I through magnificent forest. The rock and log jams start after the arch. A few require portaging. Don't mess with the log jams trying to reduce the portage by another 2m. They are some of the worst I have seen in New Zealand and would claim a life if you were swept into them. The worst of it is behind you after an hour, and a long flat stretch follows.

Within this stretch is a short gorge containing three features of note. The first is a narrowing where the river squeezes through a gap about 1m wide. The second is a drop into a sub-gorge with a big log jammed in it. Portage! Investigate the last drop, a 4m fall back into the main gorge. Either seal launch into the pool and run the drop, or portage to the bottom. A long flat section leads to New Chum and then on to Fenian Creek. Both enter from the left side. If it's raining hard, you've had enough or darkness is upon you, this is your out. Walk up Fenian Creek and take the first tributary on the right. This leads to the track that follows the main river high on the left bank. The walk out takes about an hour.

For those continuing, the paddling proper begins. The river drops away shortly after Fenian Creek. Creek-style rapids and steep boulder gardens follow with the most difficult weighing in at class V. Everything can be paddled in this last stretch. The gradient eases for the last kilometre at class II.

To get to the take out from Karamea: from the service station and shop take the road which goes straight instead of turning left towards the Last Resort. Drive along this road about four kilometres until you see a quarry site on the right. Turn in here and drive to the end of the road.

To get to the put in: continue up the Oparara Rd following signs to the Oparara Arches. Put in at the top bridge. The Last Resort offers a shuttle service that is worthwhile taking advantage of.

KARAMEA RIVER

The Karamea is sheer magic. Located in the heart of Kahurangi National Park, the huge surrounding valleys, limestone walls and enormous earthquake slips hint of powerful forces at work in the landscape, conjuring an aura hard to beat anywhere. The whitewater is fun, but don't expect a full-on 'hair' trip. People mostly come to the Karamea for its atmosphere, scenery and relaxation.

My baptism of thunder, lightning and floods on the Karamea left me with a total misconception of its beauty. We flew in for a long day trip. The river was high, thunder boomed off valley walls and the sky was thick, black and dark. The river at this level was big, pushy, and intimidating.

My next trip was from Venus Creek in low water, lots of sunshine, wine and cheese, some friends and no fixed agenda. What a difference!

The Karamea was first explored by kayak in the late 1970s. The advent of plastic boats opened up the upper reaches of the river. Now it is mostly run by commercial rafting trips offering a leisurely three or four days float from Karamea Bend. People often tramp two days into the Bend to add to the experience. Kayakers can do this too, but it takes organising to ensure that boats and food arrive at the right time.

CLASS:	III+ (IV, V)
LEVEL:	0.8 or higher
GAUGE:	at the take out on river left, or ask at Last Resort
LENGTH:	52km (Venus Ck) 38km (Karamea Bend)
GRADIENT:	6.5m/km
TIME:	2-3 days
PUT IN:	your choice
TAKE OUT:	when the river opens onto farmland
SHUTTLE:	helicopter section 7A
MAPS:	NZ Topo M27, L27
CHARACTER:	scenic beyond description, multi-day, boulder garden rapids
HOT TIP:	wine, cheese and sandfly lotion—to go

The river has been paddled from Luna Hut, but the Venus Creek put in is more common as a high put in. From Venus Creek class III rapids among scenic granite boulder gardens keep coming until Karamea Bend and the first of the earthquake lakes. From the Bend to Roaring Lion Hut is mostly flat water. Spot some BIG eels among the old rotting tree stumps in the lakes (the heaviest eel caught in the Karamea so far is 15kg!). At a big lake which looks like it has two arms, take the right arm.

Paddle as far as possible, then head across the flats on the right and look for the track to the Roaring Lion Hut.

At the end of the big lake is the first rapid. Roaring Lion is class IV+ in lower levels (<1.1 gauge) and class V- at higher flow. There are a variety of options and sneak chutes when the water is higher. Depending on the flow, rafts may take up to half a day to portage most of the rapid. Kayakers can portage on river left and consume an hour or so in the task.

A mixture of earthquake lakes and class III rapids leads to Grey's Hut. Below are a number of big granite boulder gardens. The first major rapid below the hut is Growler and the second one of note, just below the Kakapo Stream, is Holy Shit, a big class IV rapid with some equally big hydraulics to surprise folk who've relaxed into the awesome surrounds. From this last gorge are several class II and III rapids between long flat stretches down to the take out.

There are a range of choices, but I strongly recommend a multi-day trip if you want to appreciate the scenery. Putting in at Venus Creek, or higher, means at least a two day trip. Many take three days from this put in. You can arrange for a helicopter pilot to drop gear at the hut downriver so your first day is unladen. Others walk over the Wangapeka Track (two days), or come in via the Mt Arthur Tablelands (1-2 days), or fly to Karamea Bend and take two days on the river. There are one-day options too. You can be dropped just above the Roaring Lion Rapid or intermediate paddlers can be dropped at the edge of the wilderness area near Grey's Hut in the lower section. Whatever your destination, take insect repellent—the sandflies are legendary! Make sure you call in at the Last Resort for a shower and beer when you get out.

To get to the take out: from Karamea drive south towards

Westport. Turn left immediately after the Karamea bridge (Arapito Rd) and drive to the roadend. A farm gate must be left as found. Park in the grassy paddock just before a small wooden bridge. This is the usual helicopter pick up point.

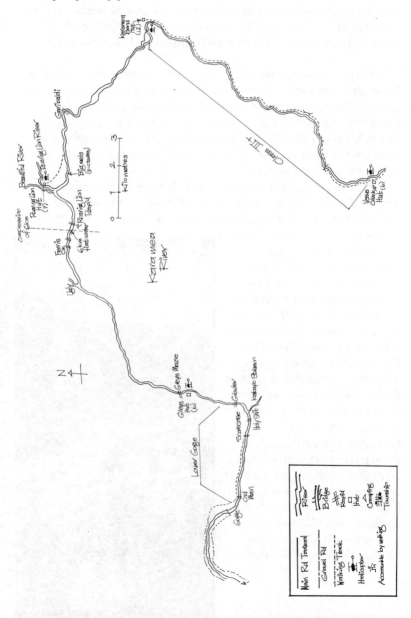

MOKIHINUI RIVER

The Mokihinui (mo-key-he-nui) was a feared river for travellers along the coastal trails from the Arahura greenstone areas. Crossing in times of flood cost lives and the trip was fraught with other dangers. An ingenious solution to these dangers gave the river its name.

A large war party from the North Island was journeying down the coast to the greenstone areas. As they travelled they were repeatedly attacked from the rear by some of the local tribes. To avoid splitting the invading party the chiefs ordered a number of kahikatea trees felled and trimmed. These were tied together with flax into a big (nui) raft (mokihi) so that the whole party could cross at the same time. The raft was left and in later times was repaired and added to by travellers going up and down the coast. It remained in use for many years*.

Any time the river is running clear it contains five or six rapids that reach class IV. All are easily portaged. The scenery is spectacular, starting at the wide open Forks and an old earthquake dam caused by the 'twenty-niner' earthquake. The first few steep rapids flow between large limestone boulders that tumbled from the surrounding hillsides at some stage in the past. These give way to even larger granite boulders and fantastic boulder garden rapids so common along the West Coast. The rapids ease after the first hour. Long, flat pools give a study in every shade of green possible.

CLASS:	III-IV
LEVEL:	any
GAUGE:	visual
LENGTH:	18.5km
GRADIENT:	6.5m/km
TIME:	3-5 hours
PUT IN:	Mokihinui Forks
TAKE OUT:	second ford after Seddonville up the Mokihinui Valley
SHUTTLE:	helicopter section 7A
MAPS:	L28
CHARACTER:	deep valley, single channel, fantastic scenery
HOT TIP:	a great first time helicopter trip

In higher flows (above 2 gauge), or when the river is running brown, expect a similar grade, but with a lot more push and less time to make decisions. The trip is much faster and requires more commitment.

To get to the take out: drive north from Westport for 44km to the small settlement at Seddonville. Take a right turn signposted to Seddonville for 2km. At a junction by the pub carry on straight, following the sealed road for another 1.7km to a farmhouse and shed. Continue past the shed on to a gravel road for 2.3km, crossing two fords. At the second ford there are good camping sites and an area for the helicopter. If the fords are uncrossable you can be picked up anywhere else, but this needs to be communicated to the pilot. Go down to the river and identify the take out spot.

* From *Greenstone Trails — The Maori search for pounamu* by Barry Brailsford.

"A Very Special Place"

BULLER RIVER
UPPER RUN

This run begins at Lake Rotoiti, the source of the mighty Buller, and is worth it if only to paddle from the lake to feel the birth of this majestic river.

From start to finish, this run is one long rapid. Make sure you are able to make an eddy to actually get out at the bridge! The section is a good beginner trip with a slightly different feel to it. As a frenetic youth working at Rotoiti Lodge in St Arnaud I paddled this section more than 150 times, mostly on my own because there was no one else to paddle with and I couldn't wait until the weekends!

To get to the take out: find the river bridge on SH63 (between St Arnaud and Kawatiri Junction) about 5km west of St Arnaud. Park river right of the bridge.

To get to the put in: head towards St Arnaud for 1.7km to the signposted turnoff to West Bay Camp Ground. Follow this gravel road for 1.3km to the bridge. Parking and river access are on the right of the bridge.

If you are after a longer run continue past the bridge, adding about 12km to the trip. The first 4km are similar to the upper run before the river eases off to class I riffles until the next access point at the Howard River on SH63.

CLASS:	II-III III+
LEVEL:	class II-III: 15-40 cumecs class III+: 40-80 cumecs
GAUGE:	visual
LENGTH:	2km
GRADIENT:	8m/km
TIME:	30-60 minutes
PUT IN:	Buller bridge on West Bay Road, Lake Rotoiti
TAKE OUT:	Buller bridge on SH63
SHUTTLE:	3.2km or run along fishing track next to the river.
MAPS:	NZ Topo N29
CHARACTER:	even gradient, single channel, bouncy fun.
HOT TIP:	there is some great mountain biking in the forest across the road

BULLER RIVER
HOWARD TO HARLEY'S ROCK

CLASS:	I-II	**TAKE OUT:**	Harley's Rock Bridge SH63
LEVEL:	any		
GAUGE:	visual	**SHUTTLE:**	5km
LENGTH:	5km	**MAPS:**	NZ Topo M29
GRADIENT:	6m/km	**CHARACTER:**	shingle braid, single channel
TIME:	40-90 minutes		
PUT IN:	800m east of Howard River Bridge SH63	**HOT TIP:**	watch for fencing wire in the river

A pleasant cruise on an ever-growing river featuring plenty of straight-shot rapids with good eddies at the bottom. The put in can be used as the take out for the upper run. The section is often used for beginner courses and club trips and can be extended by continuing to a large gravel pit a couple of kilometres past Harley's Rock Bridge. For those after something different this stretch is suitable for K1, open boats or any other recreational floating craft.

To get to the take out: SH63 runs between Kawatiri Junction and St Arnaud. About 7km east of the SH63/SH6 junction is the Harley's Rock Bridge over the Buller river.

To get to the put in: continue along SH63 for 5km to just past the Howard River Bridge and find anywhere with access to the river.

BULLER RIVER
GRANITY CREEK RUN

A nemesis for countless neophyte kayakers, spawner of numerous legends (both real and imagined), the Granity Creek section of the Buller is a classic run at any flow and one of the enduring runs in the New Zealand whitewater scene.

From the put in bouncy water keeps you busy for a couple of kilometres down to the top of Granity Creek rapid. Many get out on river right and take a look. Otherwise head down the middle and avoid the obvious hydraulics. If you are after a challenge try making as many eddies as possible down the left side of the rapid or surf the hole!

Granity Creek legends abound...in 1983 Pete Dale, then of Rotoiti Lodge, swam and lost his boat. A week later a fisherman from Westport phoned and said the mislaid kayak had been found on a sandbar at the rivermouth! Dirk Paschier attained guru status by hand paddling Granity for the first time in 1983. The Down River Racing National Champs were held on this stretch in 1986. Crowds of spectators at Granity rapid were treated to some spectacular crashes as fast moving DRR boats cannoned off walls and into holes. Long may it last.

CLASS:	III+	IV
LEVEL:	class III+: <150 cumecs	
	class IV: >150 cumecs	
GAUGE:	Tasman District Council flow phone 03 544 3393, flow at Longford	
LENGTH:	10km	
GRADIENT:	6m/km	
TIME:	2-5 hours	
PUT IN:	Gowan Bridge off SH6	
TAKE OUT:	Raits Road Bridge off SH6	
SHUTTLE:	10km	
MAPS:	NZ Topo M29	
CHARACTER:	big water, single braid	
HOT TIP:	the Owen River Pub is a great place to warm up after a trip	

Once the formalities of the main Granity Creek rapid are dispensed with, settle back for pleasant rapids and surfing through the Graveyard just below Granity. Two Mile Island is the next obvious feature with excellent eddies to carve up and play in. Just above the take out at Raits Road is a pour-over guaranteed to give good pirouette performances if your kayak is well trained.

To get to the take out: on SH6, about 22km north of Murchison is a gravel road sign posted Raits Rd. Drive 200m to the bridge. There is an alternative take out at a picnic area 2.3km after Raits Rd (heading north) which shortens the section, but keeps the excitement of Granity Creek rapids.

To get to the put in: find the turnoff to Lake Rotoroa on SH6 about 30km north of Murchison. Turn onto the gravel road and drive 200m to the bridge over the Buller River. Park either side of the bridge.

Huka Falls—awesome, inspiring, and white. Andi Uhl shows the line. (Schlegel NZ)

LEFT *The rugged beauty of the Waioeka is available to any who choose to visit. (Graham Charles)*

*The Rangitikei gorge (**above**) offers some of the North Island's classic class IV+ technical water. (Graham Charles)*

LEFT *Tilted sedimentary rock canyon in the mighty Mohaka River. (Paul Chaplow)*

Most of the rivers in Taranaki and the Central Plateau require rainfall to bring out their flavour.

ABOVE *Linda Wensley enjoys chocolate thickshake on the Mokau River. (Graham Charles)*

RIGHT *Classic pool-drop paddling on the Wairoa River. (Graham Charles)*

Surfing, playing, teaching, racing—the Buller has it all. Graham Charles takes a break from writing duties at O'Sullivans rapid. (David Bailey)

Adventure kayaking—Geoff Miles (above) exits one of the many drops on the weird and wonderful Oparara during the third descent (Graham Charles), while Peter Spiers (right) stays straight and narrow on the bent and twisted Crooked River. (Richard Sage Collection)

Many West Coast rivers cut through a band of schist bedrock before reaching the ocean. **LEFT** The entrance to the Kakapotahi Gorge.

ABOVE Jeff Sutherland tests the reality of gravity on Air Mail, Kakapotahi Gorge. (Graham Charles)

The upper sections of most West Coast rivers provide difficult kayaking conditions. The lower reaches have much to offer paddlers at all levels— Lower Gorge Kakapotahi River. (Graham Charles)

ABOVE *The massive north face of Mt Elie de Beaumont towers above the Whataroa River. The proximity of the ice fields ensure the water stays silty and cold year-round. (Graham Charles)*

LEFT *The Whitcombe River is one of the most popular West Coast runs. Dave Ritchie in Colliers Gorge. (John Imhoof)*

RIGHT *West Coast rainy days, rising rivers, big drops and bigger air on the Whataroa River. (Richard Sage Collection)*

The Arahura is sacred to the Maori for its plentiful supply of greenstone. It is sacred to kayakers for its whitewater. James Griffen gets his Curtain Call. (Graham Charles)

The author researching 'ski-jump' theory on the Wanganui. (Paul Chaplow)

ABOVE *The Perth River comes together like a well-played game of chess.*

Right, Jon Sanderson plays his way out of check. (Graham Charles)

Nevis Bluff—raw power, controlled chaos and cold objectivity—for those who dare.

RIGHT *Jeff Sutherland completes the crux of the Turnbull experience, some of the classiest class V water in New Zealand. (Graham Charles)*

ABOVE *Harsh, stark and outrageous. If he's not pushing the envelope, he's licking the stamps. Richard Sage on the Nevis River. (Peter Spiers)*

LEFT *The Hollyford rates 'number one' for many visiting kayakers. Dave Ritchie samples the delights of the big country and big water of the Marion Creek Run. (Graham Charles)*

BULLER RIVER
DOCTORS CREEK RUN

One of the most popular beginner runs in the Murchison area with great little play waves and excellent eddy lines for turns and pivots. The road runs alongside the river, but the forested river edge hides all trace and retains the 'get away from it' feel of this section. Some good holes and waves mean experienced paddlers won't be disappointed with a run in the sun on this section. Go for fun and take any boat you like.

To get to the take out: the Mangles picnic area is 4km north of Murchison on SH6. Park in the picnic area immediately after the bridge.

To get to the put in: continue north for 5.5km to 50m before the Doctors Creek bridge. There is parking on the Buller river side of the road. Walk across the paddock to the river and leave all gates as you found them.

CLASS:	II+
LEVEL:	30-150 cumecs
GAUGE:	Tasman District Council flow phone 03 544 3393, flow at Longford
LENGTH:	5.5km
GRADIENT:	3m/km
TIME:	1-3 hours
PUT IN:	across paddocks on the south side of Doctors Ck
TAKE OUT:	Mangles/Buller confluence
SHUTTLE:	5.5km
MAPS:	NZ Topo M29
CHARACTER:	big volume, single braid, great eddies
HOT TIP:	beginners delight!

137

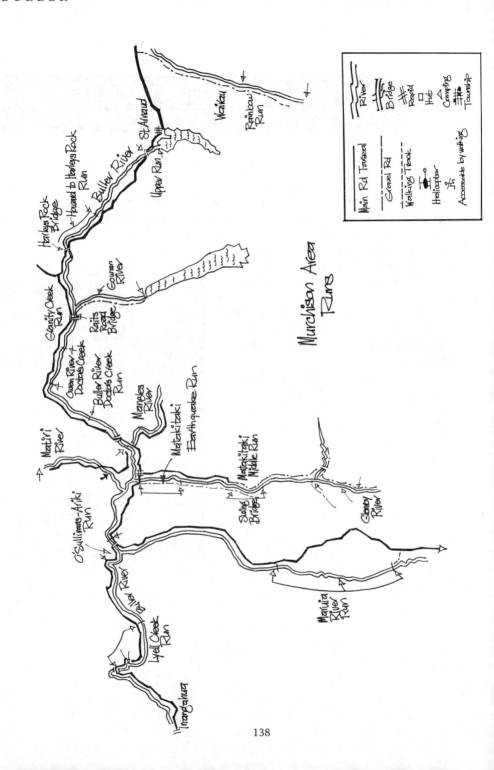

Murchison Area Runs

MANGLES RIVER

A great run for beginners and a welcome break from the wide open spaces of the Buller with lovely sunbaked rocks on which to relax and enjoy the lovely scenery. The river starts easy and gives beginners plenty of time to get warmed up. Novices should note that halfway down the run the river pours through a narrow section which will broach a boat if it is sideways. Take care!

If rain has raised other runs in the area the Mangles is definitely worth a visit from experienced paddlers.

To get to the take out: 4km north of Murchison is the Mangles bridge and picnic area. Park anywhere in the area and find the track down to the river on river right.

To get to the put in: from SH6 turn up the Mangles Valley road. Drive 5.9km to a small wooden bridge immediately before the Blackwater Creek bridge. Find the old road which leads to the river.

CLASS:	II+ (III) III-IV
LEVEL:	class II+ (III): 10-40 cumecs class III-IV: 50-150 cumecs
GAUGE:	visual
LENGTH:	6km
GRADIENT:	6m/km
TIME:	1-3 hours
PUT IN:	Blackwater Creek Bridge
TAKE OUT:	Mangles/Buller confluence
SHUTTLE:	5.9km
MAPS:	NZ Topo M29
CHARACTER:	single braid, small bedrock gorge, scenic
HOT TIP:	sandflies bite your bum when nude sunbathing!

GLENROY RIVER

The Glenroy is a well hidden Murchison secret. After rain when the Matakitaki is flowing high the Glenroy is a refreshing cure for the big water fatigue that sets in after too much of the Buller. And it's a good run for paddlers pushing into the class IV domain with a nice warm up over the first few kilometres before the final gorge with the drops that push the grade up. Three words best describe this run: short, but sweet.

CLASS:	IV+
LEVEL:	15-40 cumecs
GAUGE:	visual
LENGTH:	6km
GRADIENT:	11m/km
TIME:	1.5 hours
PUT IN:	down a small gravel road off Glenroy Valley road
TAKE OUT:	Glenroy River Bridge
SHUTTLE:	6km gravel
MAP:	NZ Topo M30
CHARACTER:	technical, short gorge
HOT TIP:	a change is as good as a holiday

The first 4.5km is open river bed, class II-III. The river enters a beautiful little gorge with a few class III rapids before the first of the two class IV drops. Both drops are worth scouting as a great deal of timber goes down this river in flood and the bottoms of the drops are invisible from the river above. They follow in quick succession and both pack a wallop. The second is the harder of the two. Both are easily portaged if need be.

To get to the take out: drive up the Matakitaki Valley from Murchison about 30km to a road junction signposted: Glenroy Valley, no exit, NLNP Entrance and Maruia Saddle. Follow the Maruia Saddle sign for 1km to the bridge crossing the Glenroy river. The take out is on river right immediately under the bridge.

To get to the put in: return to the road junction and head up the Glenroy Valley for 5km. Look for a small rocky road on the right which heads into the bush. Park and walk down the road to the river.

MATAKITAKI RIVER
MIDDLE RUN

An excellent teaching/beginner section with a special treat for the teacher—a consistently good play hole that will put a smile on the dial of even the most critical holemeister. It's one of those places to spend hours playing, hanging out and enjoying watching others paying their dues in the hole. Don't miss it.

The trip starts as a single channel over gravel river bed for a kilometre before entering a lovely gorge. The play hole is in the middle of this section. After a swingbridge the gorge gives way to open riverbed to the take out.

To get to the take out from Murchison: drive 10km up the Matakitaki Valley road. Eighty metres after the road turns to gravel, a gate on the right gives access to a farm track through a paddock to the river.

To get to the put in: continue up the valley for 5.6km to a gravel road on the right just before the second set of telephone lines across the road. Walk down to the river. Leave all gates as you find them.

CLASS:	II+
LEVEL:	most
GAUGE:	visual
LENGTH:	5km
GRADIENT:	7m/km
TIME:	1-4 hours
PUT IN:	Matakitaki Valley road by second set of telephone lines
TAKE OUT:	Matakitaki Valley road just after the road turns to gravel
SHUTTLE:	5.6km
MAPS:	NZ Topo M29, M30
CHARACTER:	single braid, good eddies, small waves and a great play hole
HOT TIP:	take lunch

MATAKITAKI RIVER
EARTHQUAKE RUN

Here's another quality short run made possible by the 1929 earthquake that sent a huge slip into the river and dammed it. Technical manoeuvring through the boulder gardens at the start of the run creates a slightly different run than many others in the region. When faced with numerous possible channels at the beginning of the run most go for the far right. Midway down, another channel joins up and this seam offers some of the best tail pivots in the area. A little further all the channels join up for the final run down the main rapid—an exciting rollercoaster ride finishing in large standing waves.

CLASS:	III+ to IV-
LEVEL:	class III+: 25-50 cumecs class IV-: 50-180 cumecs
GAUGE:	visual
LENGTH:	3.5km
GRADIENT:	8m/km
TIME:	40-60 minutes
PUT IN:	gravel road from Murchison, river left, where the road first returns to the river
TAKE OUT:	main road bridge SH6, outside Murchison
SHUTTLE:	5km
MAPS:	NZ Topo M29
CHARACTER:	tight, technical, boulder gardens
HOT TIP:	one of the most cosmopolitan take outs in the country

If you like your action dished up BIG, wait for one of the legendary Buller floods to hit the area. Get yourself to the put in and run this section a couple of times. I once did five runs in a row when the river had around 180 cumecs thundering down. I was smiling for a week! From the bottom of the earthquake rapids are several class I-II riffles. At some flows a great little play hole forms 800m up from the road bridge.

To get to the take out: leave a vehicle at the Beechwood's Restaurant! Leave some money in it for cappuccinos. Trust me.

To get to the put in: drive across the Matakitaki River bridge immediately west of Murchison and take the first road on the left. After 200m there is a fork to the right and the road changes to gravel and heads away from the river. After about 5km the road returns to the river next to a gate and old flow gauge station. Park before the gate and slide down the bank. While the shuttle is being sorted, those left over can be enjoying coffees at the café.

MATIRI RIVER

"Holy shit, I'm getting out of here," a wide-eyed Baz Simmons gasped as he rolled up in a rare eddy after being back-looped right over the top of me by a 3.5m breaking wave. Unfortunately for Baz, we were surrounded by vertical, moss-covered walls in a small gorge—the narrowest section of the Matiri. "Yeah, right Baz," sympathised the team, who then had to coax Baz into more of the non-stop maelstrom that was the Matiri in HUGE flood.

Big rains come every year to the Murchison area and the Matiri is one river that really benefits from it. The Matiri is famous for its romping stomping high flows. The days after a big rain see a throng of vehicles making their way up the valley filled with kayakers, oozing with excitement at the water they are about to meet. Basically, the higher, the better.

In flood the river moves very fast, the whole river bed moves and the short gorge produces waves up to 4m high—monsters that take your breath away and blow the minds of many first-timers to the 'joys of flood'. In these flows the rapid after the bridge is solid class IV.

In normal flows the river is a pleasant class II+ float trip through lovely bush and a short gorge. Many beginners take advantage of these conditions. The river drains Lake Matiri to the north through an impressively steep series of drops, which attracted attention in the past, but did not prove to be worthwhile.

CLASS:	III III+ to IV
LEVEL:	class III: low class III+ to IV: flood
GAUGE:	visual
LENGTH:	7.5km
GRADIENT:	8m/km
TIME:	1-3 hours
PUT IN:	Matiri Valley road end by the DOC sign
TAKE OUT:	600m below the last rapid at a small opening to the road
SHUTTLE:	7km
MAPS:	NZ Topo M29
CHARACTER:	single channel, small gorge, excellent scenery
HOT TIP:	wait for a BIG flow and don't miss out!

To get to the take out: from Murchison head north on SH6 for about 5.5km to the turnoff to the Matiri Valley. Drive 7km to the end of the seal then a further 1.2km to a small opening and access point to the river next to the road, about 1km before the bridge.

To get to the put in: continue up the valley for about 7km to the road end. Park in front of a gate and DOC sign. A small, unobvious track leads down to the river.

BULLER RIVER
O'SULLIVAN'S TO ARIKI

A classic of the Buller region, O'Sullivan's rapids are a destination in their own right used extensively for big surf sessions, slalom, rodeos and introductions to big water. Any day during summer you will find a car parked above the rapid and kayakers surfing until their arms refuse to function. Tracks provide access at the top and bottom of the rapids.

O'Sullivan's rapids were formed by a large slip that blocked the river in 1929. The area itself was named in the days when people crossed the river just up-stream of the present day SH6 bridge on a cableway.

CLASS:	III III-IV
LEVEL:	class III: <200 cumecs class: III-IV: >200 cumecs
GAUGE:	visual or TDC flow phone 03 544 3393, flow at Longford for an indication only
LENGTH:	5.9km
GRADIENT:	6m/km
TIME:	2-5 hours
PUT IN:	picnic area at the top of O'Sullivan's Rapid
TAKE OUT:	Ariki Falls (signposted) off SH6
SHUTTLE:	5km
MAPS:	NZ Topo M29
CHARACTER:	big water, bedrock gorge, single braid
HOT TIP:	Surf City

"Old Dan Sullivan would go across in the chair and up to the Fern Flat Hotel and he'd get two sheets under the weather before going home. They used to have a piece of candle that they lit and stuck in a bottle for going across at night, to see when they got to the edge. Well Dan missed his footing in the dark and he goes down the bank. He gets back to the pub about daylight and he says "The chair's in the middle of the river and I've seen the biggest star I've ever seen in my life. They get down to the river and there's only the irons dangling, the biggest star he'd seen was the chair going up in flames. The candle had burnt down and the wooden chair had caught fire." —from *Faces of the River*, by David Young and Bruce Foster, TVNZ Publishing. A bridge now stands where Dan came to grief.

After O'Sullivan's a flatwater float takes you to the confluence of the Maruia and Buller. Here the flow increases considerably, creating a section of whirly water down through Whale Creek rapid where there is good surfing at low levels. Next, Jet Boat rapid is usually run on river left against the wall, avoiding the rather aggressive hole. Ariki Falls is announced by the power lines crossing the river immediately upstream. Most parties scout before running. At lower levels when the falls are actually a fall, some consideration needs to be given to the best line. At higher levels the fall is not there at all.

Ariki was created by the 1968 Inangahua earthquake. Mike Neels was first to kayak the falls during Easter 1972. Once a test piece for any aspiring hard-kayaker, it has changed character somewhat and is now run as a matter of course by most intermediate and above teams these days. Take out at the falls or paddle 1km to the big corner past the swingbridge, then follow the track up to the road which comes out immediately across from the limeworks.

To get to the put in: O'Sullivans rapids are 10km west of Murchison alongside SH6. Park at any of the well used areas.

To get to the take out: drive a further 4.6km along SH6 and look for the signpost for Ariki Falls or continue to the limeworks.

MARUIA RIVER

The Maruia on a hot sunny day is hard to beat as a scenic, relaxing trip away from the hubbub of the popular Buller runs. It makes a great beginner/intermediate trip if a few of the harder rapids are walked.

The Maruia drains the southern Spenser Range and wends north alongside SH65 between Springs Junction and Murchison. The Shenandoah Mountains rise up to form a barrier that swings the river away from the road. The river moves west then back east to rejoin SH65 a few kilometres above Maruia Falls.

CLASS:	II-III+ IV
LEVEL:	Class II-III+: running clean Class IV: in flood
GAUGE:	visual
LENGTH:	17.5km
GRADIENT:	5m/km
TIME:	3-5 hours
PUT IN:	end of Creighton Rd (off SH65)
TAKE OUT:	Ruffe Creek bridge on SH65
SHUTTLE:	19.5km
MAPS:	NZ Topo L30
CHARACTER:	scenic, wilderness, single braid fun
HOT TIP:	a great 'get away from it' day

The run begins as easy class II riffles for a few kilometres until well away from the road. The beech forest crowding down to the water's edge is stunning. This, combined with crystal clear water and an abundance of fish and game, means that the most common visitors to the area are hunters and anglers. The few harder rapids are in the steeper areas with big boulders in the river. The paddling here is very enjoyable, and at very high flows the large waves that are kicked up keep you guessing at what's over the lip right to the finish. Towards the end the river enters a short gorge typical of the region. Once clear of this a kilometre or so of class I water will see you at the take out and road.

To get to the put in: find Creightons Rd off SH65 about 18km north of Springs Junction. Drive 2km down this gravel road to the barn and gate at the end of the road. A small stream runs alongside the road just by the gate. Follow this stream 150m to its confluence with the Maruia. Make sure that any vehicles left at the put in are well off the roadway, and ensure all gates and fences are left as they are found. Access is via a paper road.

To get to the take out: the take out is on the northern side of Shenandoah Saddle on SH65. The easiest parking area is at Ruffe Creek, where the Maruia returns to the road. There are small tracks through the bush to the river.

Maruia Falls is downstream about 15km. The falls were paddled for the first time in 1983 by Mick Hopkinson and Gillian Wratt. Many have followed in their wake. Don't be too casual, at least four people have been hospitalised with compressed vertebrae from landing flat in the pool below. Others have also spent time behind the curtain of water while spectators were stressed out because the kayaker had disappeared for so long. Make sure you take a photo then look at the transparency around the wrong way, then look in the Nepal *Whitewater* guidebook for the 'sandbag falls' that are actually in New Zealand!

Mick Hopkinson, kayaking guru. (Graham Charles)

BULLER RIVER
EARTHQUAKE RUN

Great scenery, great surfing, great sandflies, home of the great Whopper Stopper and Gunslinger, inspiration for great tales in the Murchison pub... one of the all time great runs.

CLASS:	III IV
LEVEL:	class III: <200 cumecs
	class IV: >200 cumecs
GAUGE:	visual
LENGTH:	10km
GRADIENT:	6m/km
TIME:	2-5 hours
PUT IN:	Harry's Track carpark
TAKE OUT:	Iron Bridge SH6
SHUTTLE:	12km
MAPS:	NZ Topo M29
CHARACTER:	big water, single braid
HOT TIP:	Gunslinger is the greatest

Earthquake is named for the 1929 quake that sent a huge slip down the south bank into the river. This monster dammed the river dry for 48 hours causing major concern it would burst and obliterate everything in its path. Fortunately, it released slowly. The remains of the slip create a lake at the put in and a gentle introduction to the awesome run that follows.

Big riffles appear well before Whopper Stopper, but the rock that caused the hydraulic and gave the rapid its name has rolled over and tends not to form the whopper stopper of legend. At higher flows there are some excellent catch-on-the-fly surf waves. Rodeo Rapid, underneath a big eroded corner, is the place to surf at low flows. Slide, a big straight shot rapid with large pressure waves, leads into the gorge proper.

The eddies in this pivot paradise have developed a taste for kayakers and their equipment. One unfortunate swimmer in this boil and whirlpool heaven was struggling through a lengthy session in the green room. Between gasps while surfacing he managed to communicate to his rescuers that his beloved socks had just been sucked off his feet. Long live the Sock Sucker!

Gunslinger, the climax of the run, will bring smiles to the biggest of big-water freaks. Often there's a superb surf wave right at the top, while the rapid itself is a series of huge waves and hydraulics. As flow increases the waves just keep getting bigger, as do the grins and the eyes. As with all 'good' things (unlike things which are 'good for you') it's over too soon and the age old Kiwi kayakers' lament begins: "If only it went on for .....". Surf and enjoy from here to the take out. Keep an eye open for a little ender spot 600m above the Lyell Creek confluence—a pour-over against a rock in an unlikely looking spot on river right.

To finish, either get out and walk up Lyell Creek, or float the mostly flat water to the old Iron Bridge across the Buller.

To get to the put in: from Murchison, check your odometer, drive 29.2km and find a gravel road that turns sharply down to the left after a sweeping right hand corner (marked by a 60km speed sign. This is Harry's Track, which provides rough access to the carpark 200m down.

To get to the take out: return to SH6 and continue west to either Lyell Creek or, more commonly, the old Iron Bridge. Turn right immediately before the bridge and drive down a gravel road to a turn-around area.

GREY RIVER
GENTLE ANNIE GORGE

An excellent scenic, moderate trip for strong beginners. Great eddies and scenery offer a fun half-day trip, or take lunch (and sandfly repellent) and make a day of it. Low volume boats will find plenty of squirting and playing through the gorge.

To get to the put in from Ikamatua: drive north on SH7 for 3km to a road signposted Hukarere immediately before the Snowy Creek bridge. Turn right onto this and drive 29km on a single lane, gravel road to a creek down to the river. If you get to a house and private property sign you have gone 150m too far. Carry down the bank and across the river flats to the river.

To get to the take out: return to Ikamatua and drive south over the Big Grey River bridge. About 200m after the bridge, turn left at a sign to: Waipuna No Exit. Follow this road for 16.5km, over two bridges, to anywhere with access to the river. Leave gates as you find them.

The upper Grey area creates the option of a multi-day, moderate trip starting south of Springs Junction. This starts on the northern branch (Blue Grey) and goes down to the junction with the Grey. Most parties continue and camp somewhere before the Gentle Annie Gorge, then finish at Waipuna Rd the next day.

CLASS:	III
LEVEL:	60-150 cumecs
GAUGE:	NIWA Greymouth 03 768 0390. Ask for the flow on the Grey at Waipuna
GRADIENT:	5m/km
LENGTH:	15km
TIME:	2-4 hours
PUT IN:	end of gravel road on river right
TAKE OUT:	river access point off Waipuna Rd
SHUTTLE:	49km
MAPS:	NZ Topo L31
CHARACTER:	single channel, moderate, good eddy lines
HOT TIP:	drive carefully into the put in, the road is very narrow and winding

CROOKED RIVER
UPPER GORGE

What a run. It's hard to categorise this one, but it must be done if you're in the area and have the skills to do it. Many claim it's the best run they have done, though it's difficult to pinpoint why. The water is crystal clear in the shallows and aqua blue in the pools. The boating is fun, though short. The canyon is spectacular. It is probably a combination of these that turns people on to this one, and erases the pain of sore shoulders, the mud and slippery tree roots on the two hour walk in.

The Crooked River is just north of SH73 between Arthur's Pass and Greymouth. It flows west from the Kaimata Range and ends its life on the eastern side of Lake Brunner. On the water you have 200m to warm up before the first drop. Once in the gorge there is no backing out and all portages are difficult. Good boat-scouting and boofing skills are a prerequisite.

Five drops down is Bent and Twisted, the crux rapid with a difficult lead into a steep and narrow chute, with an ugly run out and a must-make boof move to finish. Sound like fun? Once this formality is dispensed with, either through good boating skills or staunch portaging on a ledge high above river left, there are two more class IV drops before the intensity eases.

CLASS:	IV+ to V
LEVEL:	10-15 cumecs
GAUGE:	water level needs to be below the bedrock/ concrete interface under the old bridge piles on the river left
LENGTH:	2.5km
GRADIENT:	28m/km
TIME:	40 minutes-4 hours
PUT IN:	where the track first returns to the river (see accompanying map)
TAKE OUT:	at the old bridge site
SHUTTLE:	walk or Helicopter section 7B
MAPS:	NZ Topo K32
CHARACTER:	stunning schist canyon, steep, pool-drop rapids
HOT TIP:	calf, as in small cow, deep mud!

To get to the take out: find the road between Jacksons (SH73) and Stillwater (SH7), get to the T-junction southeast of Rotomanu. From the junction head northeast for just over 2km. There is a farmhouse on the right about 100m off the road. Collect the key for locked gate from here (phone Bruce Burgess, 03 738 0177, to arrange key). A further 800m after the farmhouse there is a gravel road on the right with one very rough section in the first 100m known for damaging vehicles. The remaining 2.8km to the old bridge are fine. Please leave all gates and electric fences as found. The farmer has requested that people don't run or bike through the farm track as this spooks the cattle more than vehicles. Please abide by this.

To get to the put in: from the take out find the start of the track in the bush behind the Otira Kopara sign. Walk, slush, grovel and fight your way for about two hours to where the track returns to the river after a climb away from it. You can walk further up if you want to.

In 1996 Richard Sage, Pete Speirs, Dave Ritchie and Jon Sanderson flew into the Forks Hut and made their way out from there. Conditions were reported as very steep and crooked. They managed a paddle/ portage ratio of about 60/40.

There is also a lovely class II-III run on the lower Crooked. Put in at the old bridge site (take out for the upper run) and paddle about 4.5km to the first road bridge over the Crooked. This short schist gorge is a popular beginner trip and well worthwhile.

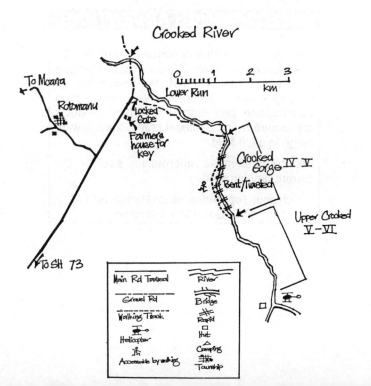

TAIPO RIVER

The Taipo, meaning monster or taniwha, was so-named because it claimed the lives of many Maori who travelled through the area. One story also claims the name was coined because the water was so cold it felt as though a monster had grabbed the loins of those crossing.

The Taipo is one of the best adventure river runs in the country. It offers stunning scenery and location, excellent whitewater and good length. The lower 3km through the short, scenic gorge has been used by kayakers and rafters for several years and is a good day out if you are new to the Coast and at a loss for something to do. Kayakers began flying up the valley to Tumbledown Stream in 1993. They returned with stories of amazing water and wild experiences. Bruce Barnes et al went higher to paddle from Julia Hut and produced a mega-classic. Above Julia Hut the river divides and the lack of volume will restrict exploration to times when there is plenty of water in the main river.

From the first breakout at Julia Hut the action is fast and busy—6km of continuous whitewater with only small eddies to rest in. Entrance Exam—a class IV+ drop in the first 2km—has a pushy hydraulic at the bottom that will take most by surprise. A kilometre below Tumbledown Stream is a short gorge with two hard-to-scout class IV+ rapids—Tit and Tat. If anyone in your party is struggling it would be a good idea to portage the whole gorge on the track on river right. A further 800m, just above Dexter Creek, is the biggest, steepest rapid on the river. Showcase—a solid class V multi-tiered drop—is split into two sections. The first and crucial drop can be paddled, but many will take the sneak route down the right. Below is another big drop into a pool. A pushy S bend leads to more moderate class IV water. Scouting is easiest

CLASS:	IV+ (V)
LEVEL:	2.8-3.2 gauge
GAUGE:	at the take out or phone NIWA Greymouth 03 768 0390
LENGTH:	23km
GRADIENT:	35m/km in first 6km, 13m/km for remainder
TIME:	5-8 hours
PUT IN:	Julia Creek Hut
TAKE OUT:	Taipo Rd Bridge SH73
SHUTTLE:	helicopter section 7B
MAPS:	NZ Topo K33
CHARACTER:	steep, technical, busy water, very scenic, classic test piece
HOT TIP:	Westpower want to build a dam on this!! Don't let it happen

from the right as is the ensuing portage for many.

You can be dropped off at Tumbledown Stream, allowing an easier warm-up for a kilometre or so instead of the intensity of the Julia Hut put in.

At Mid Taipo Hut the gradient eases markedly into 13km of class II-III boulder gardens through open valley flats to the last gorge and the road bridge. If flows are very high (>3.4 gauge) this section on its own is a lot of fun and gets into class IV at flows around 4 on the gauge.

The length and difficulty of the entire run makes it a very serious proposition. Make sure the weather forecast is solid and be conscious of the time. A strong team will get down in 4-5 hours, but with time spent scouting and portaging, many will take 7-8 hours.

To get to the take out: find the Taipo River Bridge on SH73. On the upstream side of the bridge on river right is a gate into a clearing. Park there and leave room for the helicopter. To access the lower gorge drive east from the bridge for 1km and look for a road on the right marked Taipo Valley Access. This rough, steep road climbs over the first gorge. Unless you have four wheel drive, park at the top of the hill and walk down to the river.

Upper Taipo

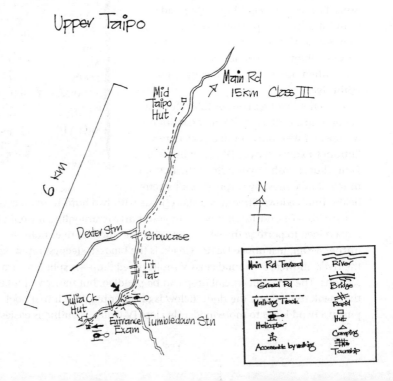

ARAHURA RIVER

A must for any West Coast hair boating aficionado, the Arahura is one of the very best runs in New Zealand with a wide range of runnable flow levels, great scenery, wild location and stunning whitewater.

In 1986 Hugh Canard and two companions made what is thought to be the first kayak descent beginning near Olderog Creek. In 1993 Bruce Barnes investigated and ran the third gorge. By the end of that season at least four other teams had sampled the delights of the Upper Arahura. In 1994 Bruce and Mick Hopkinson et al flew in through Styx Saddle and paddled from the top of the river, adding a class III+ section that hasn't seen much action since then. Most parties continue to put in at the top of what is known as the third gorge.

Busy class III-IV rock gardens lead into the third gorge. Five hundred metres in is Curtain Call—a pour-over with a curtain of water on the right side. Get airborne and boof on the right, or portage. Two hundred metres further is Dent Falls—a thundering cauldron at high flows, or a possible piton spot in low flows. Do what you will, but scouting and portaging are easiest on river right. Below Dent Falls the intensity eases briefly until Olderog Creek. (There is a hut here).

CLASS:	IV-V (VI-, P)
LEVEL:	running clean
GAUGE:	visual
LENGTH:	15.2km
GRADIENT:	21m/km (36m/km first 5km)
TIME:	4.5-8 hours
PUT IN:	above third gorge near Newton Creek
TAKE OUT:	Arahura Bridge above Milltown
SHUTTLE:	helicopter section 7B
MAPS:	NZ Topo K33, J33
CHARACTER:	steep, tight, technical
HOT TIP:	whenever you sin, sin with a grin

Tight class IV+ water leads into the second gorge and a very steep, unlikely-looking rapid called Billiards. This has been run top to bottom in low flows, but most portage the top 50m. At higher flows it is possible to sneak down channels on river left and pop into the rapid halfway down to finish off. Below Billiards a few drops will cause most parties to scout, but conditions ease considerably for 2-3km before the Cesspit.

If you've already decided against the final gorge, the track is on river left about 150m before the gorge starts. If you venture to the top of the

Cesspit make sure you get out on the left well before the drop into it. Having scouted, oohed and aahed, and decided not to run the class VI-entrance rapid, carry boats up the small stream at the very top of the gorge to the track. Nearly 1km of walking will see you back at the river for the final few kilometres of class II-III water to the take out.

The Cesspit has a number of possible variations. All of it has been paddled except the mandatory portage around a rock sieve 200m into the gorge. Drop into the top of the gorge from river right, sliding over the lip of the falls for a 4m boof. Then "hold on to your hat" says Richard Sage, who has run it twice—twice more than most. Get yourself and your hat to the must-make eddy on the right and climb around the sieve. Slide back into the water for two more class IV drops. (To avoid the class VI- entrance, you can seal launch off a big rock into the bottom of the first rapid, cross immediately to the must-make eddy and go from there.)

To get to the take out: follow signs from Hokitika to Lake Kaniere. From the foot of the lake continue for 1km to a gravel road on the left signposted No Exit, Milltown. Follow this road for 9.7km to a bridge over the Arahura. Park on river right and leave room for the helicopter.

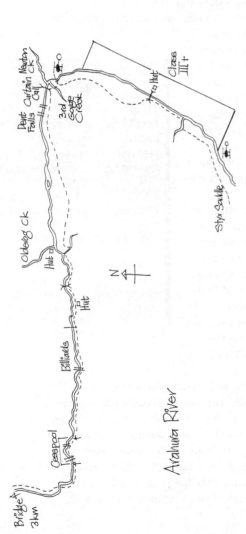

TOAROHA RIVER

The Toaroha, a tributary of the Kokatahi River, has been popular with Coast boaters for some time. Flowing out of the Alps, it cuts through a gorge in a small area of schist bedrock east of Hokitika. After rain the Toaroha is a fast, rolling run, pushing into class V, and during normal flows it offers superb class III-IV boulder gardens.

There are two options: walk for 50 minutes along an old tram track for an enjoyable run with good playing, or for a longer, harder run, fly to the bottom of Toaroha Canyon by helicopter. Costs are reasonable as it is on the back doorstep of the Hokitika operators.

To get to the take out: from Hokitika follow signs to Kokatahi. At the road junction at Kokatahi turn left onto Upper Kokatahi Rd. Follow the road for 11km crossing the Styx River on the way. Take the first right after the Styx bridge, signposted Toaroha Valley Access. Follow 3km of gravel road which crosses the Kokatahi River after 1km. At the end is a locked gate. The road from here is 4WD. Park on the side of the road and leave room for the helicopter.

The 50 minute walk in: follow the 4WD road down to the river and look for track markers heading away from the river, up into the bush. This wide tram track rejoins the river at a cliff. Turn right and bush bash downriver 100m to a beach.

CLASS:	III-IV (V)
LEVEL:	class III-IV: most class (V): flood
GAUGE:	visual
GRADIENT:	20m/km
LENGTH:	5m/km
TIME:	1-3 hours
PUT IN:	below Toaroha Canyon
TAKE OUT:	when the river hits farmland and the 4WD track drops onto the river flats
SHUTTLE:	helicopter section 7B (or 50min walk for a shorter run)
MAPS:	NZ Topo J33
CHARACTER:	steep, moderate, boulder gardens
HOT TIP:	a lovely walk

KOKATAHI RIVER

I'd definitely caught the adventure kayaking bug during the guidebook tour of 1996. Bruce Barnes and I had spent a great deal of time poring over maps and books. The Kokatahi remained an enigma. Bruce had tramped the valley, but the track climbed 400m above the river making river investigation impossible. The reason for the climb was that the lower river region was rugged and steep. This piqued our interest even more. The pilot from Kokatahi reckoned most of the river looked a go, but it had three tight gorges. He offered a free recce trip to scope it from the air. We flew the river three times and saw mostly hard, but feasible whitewater. We decided to do it.

CLASS:	IV-V (VI-, P)
LEVEL:	6-12 cumecs at the put in
GAUGE:	visual
LENGTH:	13km
GRADIENT:	26m/km (40m/km 3km section through middle)
TIME:	6-8 hours
PUT IN:	Crawford Junction
TAKE OUT:	bridge at the pick-up point
SHUTTLE:	helicopter section 7B
MAPS:	NZ Topo J33
CHARACTER:	steep, tight, technical
HOT TIP:	do not attempt the first gorge

Just a few hundred metres of class II-III rock gardens from the put in, the river drops away from under you. The next few kilometres are mostly runnable class IV+ to V, typical Coast water with a couple of portages. Don't run anything you can't see the bottom of. The only drop of particular note is Cover Shot—an absolutely awesome looking 4m drop that I was convinced would be the cover shot for the guidebook. I took a pile of photos, but they were subsequently lost and I never got back to re-shoot. It is a 4m fall between two hotel-sized boulders, requiring a couple of moves during the lead-in to line up and boof into the pool.

Walking time arrives when the schist walls of Carnage Gorge stand before you. On no account enter the gorge itself!! Take out on the left and find the marked route up and over the gorge. This portage is an hour of hard work, so shoes will save a great deal of pain.

Back on the water the intensity remains, but the rapids change character. Rather than being amorphous steep water, they separate and become single entities. Each contains a series of complex moves to a short break. All are portageable with a bit of investigation as to the best line.

The second gorge looms large and is an easy float for 100m. Take out on the left to portage around a big waterfall immediately after. It needs rope work to lower boats off the big boulder and back to river level. Without boats it is possible to climb around on the slabs, otherwise climb a short way into the bush.

Class V water and more portages keep you honest through Whakarira Gorge. Class II breaks between are a welcome respite. One section of complex rapids in this schist gorge has not been paddled, as of 1996. The easiest portage is on ledges at the bush edge on river right.

The intensity eases slightly until Adamson Creek joins the river at the top left of the last gorge and an obvious class V rapid. In this gorge you are committed to one more class V drop. If you opt to portage find the track, which comes down to river level at Adamson Creek. Follow this up and over the gorge, across a swingbridge and find a point to get back in the river. Below this gorge to the take out is class II.

Whoever or whatever you are, the Kokatahi is a tough day out. Make sure all your team are well prepared for adventure in every sense of the word.

To get to the take out: from Hokitika follow signs to Kokatahi. At the road junction at Kokatahi turn left onto Upper Kokatahi Rd. Drive for 11km, crossing the Styx River on the way. Turn right on the first road after the Styx bridge, signposted Toaroha Valley Access. Drive 1km to the Kokatahi bridge.

To get to the put in: fly to Crawford Junction.

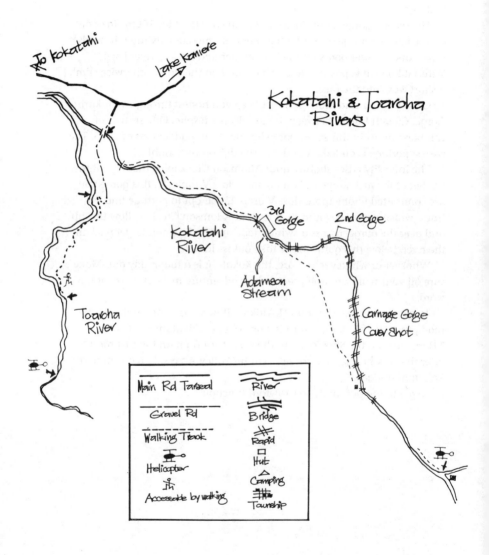

Kokatahi & Toaroha
Rivers

To Kokatahi

Lake Kaniere

Kokatahi
River

3rd Gorge

2nd Gorge

Adamson
Stream

Toaroha
River

Carnage Gorge
Cover Shot

Main Rd Tarseal

River

Gravel Rd

Bridge

Walking Track

Rapid

Helicopter

Hut

Accessible by walking

Camping

Township

WHITCOMBE RIVER

The Whitcombe makes it into many kayakers' top five ratings for New Zealand river trips. It carries more water than your average Coast steep creek so feels like a 'real' river.

It was very much a real river for Henry Whitcombe and Douglas Lauper in 1865 when they crossed Whitcombe Pass from the Rakaia and pioneered a route down the valley. They figured on an easy journey so were carrying meagre rations. Instead it took them 14 days from the top of the pass to the coast, plagued by rough travel, rain, cold, lack of food and sandflies. They arrived at the coast and stumbled north to find the Maori pa at the Taramakau. When they tried to ford the flooded Taramakau, Whitcombe was swept away to 'the great New Zealand death'. Lauper later recovered his body—still attached to a boot poking out of a sandbank.

Recreational river use started with New Zealand's first hair boating movie shot on 35mm by Gary Rae (on inner tube), Graham Boddy (in a dory), and Graham Hamilton rowing a single-person raft. This movie sparked a lot of the early interest in the potential of the West Coast.

From the put in at Cropp River conflu-ence, the paddling starts gently with superb class III+ boulder gardens. The odd class IV+ rapid maintains interest and prepares you for Colliers Gorge. A swingbridge heralds the entrance to the gorge and the gradient increases to 31m/km, adding to the overall ambience. If this section is not your cup of tea then portage on the track up on the left side.

Chicane Rapid is the entrance to Colliers Gorge with large hydraulics to trip you up. Good play holes on Staircase lead down to a short pool.

CLASS:	IV+ (V) V
LEVEL:	class IV+ (V): 20-100 cumecs class V: >100 cumecs
GAUGE:	visual at the take out (allow for the Hokitika flow in here as well, approx $1/4$)
LENGTH:	12.5km
GRADIENT:	14m/km
TIME:	4-5 hours
PUT IN:	Cropp River Junction
TAKE OUT:	second Cableway in the Hokitika
SHUTTLE:	helicopter section 7B
MAPS:	NZ Topo J34
CHARACTER:	big boulder gardens with a big water feel, especially in Colliers Gorge
HOT TIP:	never turn down a trip on the Whitcombe

Corridor is the crux, difficult to scout and shoots you straight into Pinball. This has a number of aggressive holes, rocks and other such features we hate when we're being worked by them, but we dream of when we're at work. It's a strange sport.

Below the gorge are a couple of other class IV drops before the Hokitika confluence, then an easy paddle to the take out just after the cableway. During summer 1996, a group of sledgers swam and sledged from the Cropp put in.

To get to the take out: follow signs from Hokitika to Kokatahi. From here follow signs to Hokitika Gorge. Shortly after the road comes close to the Hokitika River there is a side road on the left posted Whitcombe Valley Access. Follow this to its end at the old hut site and take out/pick up. The road is very rough with one culvert that occasionally washes out. The helicopter pilot should be able to provide an update on road conditions. If the road is unsuitable the pick up/take out is at the bottom of the Hokitika Gorge. Allow an hour from Hokitika to pick up time.

The normal put in is on a sandbar at the confluence of the Cropp River and Whitcombe rivers. You can fly much higher up the Whitcombe and do a two day trip. This is an exciting class IV-V run with one long portage around the gorge just above the Cropp River. It could be done in a very long day.

Bruce Barnes renowned
Hokitika canoeist

HOKITIKA RIVER
(KAKARIKI CANYON)

The Hokitika is rafted commercially and makes an ideal first helicopter trip. Once at the put in it is possible to carry boats upstream right to the bottom of Kawau Gorge for a few extra drops and fantastic photographs in the clear blue water.

Begin with some eddy hopping through class III boulder gardens into a short, scenic, waterworn granite gorge perfect for stunning photographs. The river opens to a long boulder garden of slip debris that changes regularly. It is generally class IV easing to class III at the Hokitika/ Whitcombe confluence. At higher flows, greater than 40 cumecs, the whole trip is a pumping rollercoaster ride, but is so quick you'll be wondering if it was worth the cost of the chopper. At any flow this is a short trip and you'll have energy left to make the most of the two play holes below the confluence. Late summer flows below 15 cumecs make the trip not worth doing.

The upper Hokitika has kilometres of excellent water, but the intermittent gorges are unknown quantities. Landing spots are scarce and thorough helicopter reconnaissance would be needed to scope this out properly.

The put in is on a gravel bar below Kawau Gorge.

The take out/pick up is as for the Whitcombe.

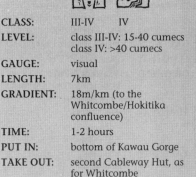

CLASS:	III-IV IV
LEVEL:	class III-IV: 15-40 cumecs class IV: >40 cumecs
GAUGE:	visual
LENGTH:	7km
GRADIENT:	18m/km (to the Whitcombe/Hokitika confluence)
TIME:	1-2 hours
PUT IN:	bottom of Kawau Gorge
TAKE OUT:	second Cableway Hut, as for Whitcombe
SHUTTLE:	helicopter section 7B
MAPS:	NZ Topo J34
CHARACTER:	small water technical, lots of moves around big schist boulders, beautiful scenic gorge
HOT TIP:	take a camera

KAKAPOTAHI RIVER

The beautiful, tight, granite upper gorge of the Kakapotahi is one of the most fun novelty runs on the West Coast. It has seven drops, all of which are very hard to scout, with penalties for making mistakes. Finding someone with prior experience is a good idea, especially if the river is pushing the upper end of the flow level. Twelve cumecs is optimal and requires rain to get to this level. The two middle drops are the hardest. Run Postman's Falls hard left. The following Air Mail rapid is run down the middle to the big rock, then boofed pointing left to avoid the rock that's waiting for more plastic to be smeared on it.

It is crucial to gain information on this run before you go. A little too much water and you are in for a portage fest that will test your ingenuity and rope skills to the max. After each flood a great deal of timber comes down the stream. If you are the first down after such an event, treat the run as a new one because this canyon traps logs from time to time. If the top section is all the excitement you want, take out at the put in for the lower run.

The lower gorge is more fun with extra water in it, but can be paddled at most flows. After the class IV descent to the put in there are some good warm-up class II rapids before the river sidles into an innocuous looking gorge. Get out on river right and scramble up past a swingbridge to a good vantage point where a small stream runs through a break in the granite walls. This drop is the hardest in the bottom section and is a Class IV+ to V depending on the flow. Portage on river right to the bottom of the little gorge or take a deep breath and run the drop.

The tempo doesn't ease for 2.5km as you negotiate fantastic granite

CLASS:	IV+ to V
LEVEL:	8-20 cumecs (upper gorge), any level for the lower gorge
GAUGE:	visual, or local beta
LENGTH:	9km
GRADIENT:	40m/km for first kilometre, 10m/km for the rest of the run
TIME:	4-8 hours
PUT IN:	either mid-gorge or top-gorge
TAKE OUT:	Kakapotahi road bridge on SH6
SHUTTLE:	8-9.5km
MAPS:	NZ Topo I34
CHARACTER:	very tight, technical, committing, photogenic, sheer granite gorge
HOT TIP:	this would make a great advertisement for New Zealand Post!

boulder garden rapids (around class IV) through spectacular moss-covered granite sub-gorges. Then the river spills onto an open plain for the final stretch to the road bridge.

To get to the take out: from Hokitika drive 40km south to the SH6 bridge over the Kakapotahi river. Park on the south side.

To get to the put in: drive 500m south from the Kakapotahi and turn left up the Mikonui Forest Rd (unsealed). One kilometre up this road is a sometimes-locked gate and another 6km to an obvious cleared area. (Be careful at a Y-junction a couple of kilometres past the gate—stay on the right.) The put in for the lower run is down the grassy/mud slope leading out of the clearing. For the top gorge, drive a further 1.5km to where the valley opens out. Park in an open area just before the road meets the river. The first drop, Mail Box, can be scouted down a faint track into the bush on the left of the clearing that leads to an old bridge site high above the river. If the gate is locked the key may be obtained from Sam Tapp (03 755 4087) who lives in the small community of Kakapotahi just north of the Waitaha road bridge on SH6.

WANGANUI RIVER

The character of the Wanganui is different from other West Coast rivers, dropping sharply out of the Alps, but easing off without flowing through any gorges. From just above the Lambert/Wanganui junction is a great class III intermediate trip and an excellent proposition for a first helicopter trip. Those flying higher will be treated to some excellent, technical boating that at first glance looks unlikely, but comes together with a bit of thought and a few forced errors. Be aware that this streambed is highly mobile and large floods can change the nature of the rapids completely. There are too many rapids to point out any one line so I will leave it up to you to adventure, or misadventure, at your own leisure.

CLASS:	IV-V
LEVEL:	30-80 cumecs
GAUGE:	visual at the take out
GRADIENT:	35-40m/km in first 3km, 9.5m/km from Lambert Junction to take out
TIME:	4.5-6 hours
PUT IN:	Hunters Hut (Wanganui/ Lambert confluence) or 5km further upstream at any available landing spot
TAKE OUT:	gravel roadend 3km up from SH6 (right side)
SHUTTLE:	helicopter section 7B or 7C
MAPS:	NZ Topo I34, J34
CHARACTER:	steep, technical to open moderate water
HOT TIP:	a great intermediate trip from Lambert Junction

After five kilometres of steep water the gradient drops right off to 9.5m/km for the rest of the trip and enjoyable class III water, except for one class IV-V rapid. This rapid (Slip Rapid) is about 4km from the Lambert/Wanganui junction and is easy to spot from above. Run the rapid or portage on the left side.

A soak in the hot pools in Hot Spring Stream (on the left 2km before the take out) is a great way to finish the trip. Walk 100m up the stream on the true left and dig out a pool to sit in. The quarry site on river right indicates the take out 200m further on.

To get to the take out: from Harihari drive south until you are about to cross the Wanganui River. The old road turns off left and heads up the valley. Follow this for about three kilometres. Just as the road gets to the river there is a good parking and landing area.

To get to the put in: fly to the Wanganui/Lambert river confluence.

PERTH RIVER

OUTRAGEOUS is the only word to describe the first 3km of the Perth. It is about as steep as it comes in New Zealand and makes for a superb day. The scenery is stunning, the water is cold and the paddling totally absorbing. After my first run on the Perth I remembered only one rapid that stood out from the rest and that was because we walked it.

Olaf Koehler from Wyoming pushed high up the river to Scone Hut in 1994 and produced a stunner. The lower river from Five Finger Stream has been paddled since 1990. For those wanting to see the area and still enjoy some good class IV action, this makes a great put in and still leaves the remaining 9km of the Perth and the last 6km of the Whataroa to the road bridge.

Once unloaded near Scone Hut, check out the scenery—the mountains at the head of the Perth are fantastic. On the water you have a kilometre or so to connect all your motor neurons and fast-twitch muscles before the gradient increases. The next 2km is one steep, long rapid. From the helicopter it looks unlikely and in need of a full 2km scouting mission. But once into it most can be scouted from the boat, assuming you have the skills to be there in the first place!

CLASS:	V (VI)
LEVEL:	40-160 cumecs
GAUGE:	Greymouth NIWA 03 768 0390. Ask for the Whataroa gauge and halve this for the Perth
LENGTH:	13km
GRADIENT:	20, 40, 50m/km for the first 3km, 18m/km average from there
TIME:	4-6 hours
PUT IN:	Scone Hut
TAKE OUT:	old road SH6 bridge on Whataroa River
SHUTTLE:	helicopter section 7B or 7C
MAPS:	NZ Topo I35
CHARACTER:	tight, technical, very steep, lots of moves around big schist boulders. Very scenic
HOT TIP:	a range of trips for many levels

The run slowly unravels like a well-played chess game until near Five Finger Stream. A steep drop onto a large rock—Pinballs—has put people off to date, but there is a runnable class IV sneak line on river right. Soon after, a large slip on river left heralds Knuckle Grinder. This steep little class VI- teaser is a result of some big floods in 1995. The line is all there

169

on the left side (watch your elbows), but don't stray off it or trouble ensues in the form of a huge boulder that the water apparently flows underneath and is squeezed out in smaller molecules—I kid you not.

The intensity eases after here and you can relax into class III+ water for a few kilometres past Nolan's Hut until the final gorge. This is a stunning, smooth, schist-walled gorge well worth getting the camera out for. It contains four or five class IV rapids. The Weir is an obvious river-wide waterfall/slide thingy which many people portage, but it has been run on a variety of lines at a variety of levels.

Once clear of the gorge the confluence with the Whataroa arrives quickly. Six kilometres of leisurely floating takes you down to the old bridge site, carpark, beers and sandflies. Load up your gear as quickly as possible and head south for 5km to the small township of Whataroa. Locate the Whataroa tearooms in the central business district and treat yourself to Bill's scones with lashings of whipped cream and jam. They are hard to beat and the best buy on the Coast.

Perth River

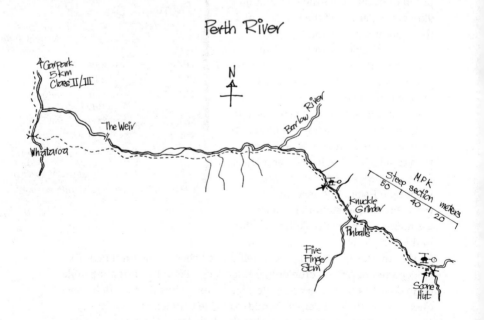

WHATAROA RIVER

The upper Whataroa scenery is spectacular, but you may not notice it. The huge north face of Mt Elie de Beaumont provides a stunning backdrop for the first couple of kilometres, but the only problem is there's not much opportunity to stop and look at anything except the next difficult rapid.

The first kilometres pack plenty of punch and are the crux of the Whataroa experience. This is a river that feels 'big'. Like the Whitcombe, the moves are often complex *and* huge and the water is silty and cold, all of which doesn't add up to having a relaxing time. If you aren't prepared to get scared and paddle some big, hard drops, don't bother flying in. This is not a creek.

The action starts with busy, large rapids steep enough that you can't see the bottom and they require scouting. Most have a route somewhere that will only become apparent after scouting or brave eddy hopping. About 2km down is a large rapid that has probably been walked more than it has been paddled. There is a line. Just decide for yourself. If you portage, the track close by on the right up a side stream offers the quickest route to the bottom of the rapid.

CLASS:	IV+ (V)
LEVEL:	40-120 cumecs (roughly 60 per cent the flow from the NIWA gauge)
GAUGE:	visual, or NIWA Greymouth 03 768 0390
LENGTH:	16.8km
GRADIENT:	28.5m/km first 3km, 8m/km from there
TIME:	3.5-5 hours
PUT IN:	Butler Hut or Barrowman Flat
TAKE OUT:	old SH6 bridge site
SHUTTLE:	helicopter section 7B or 7C
MAPS:	NZ Topo I35
CHARACTER:	big boulder gardens, big water feel
HOT TIP:	fly to Barrowman Flat and take a play boat

Keep your eyes peeled for the approaching Portals of Doom and the swingbridge. Take out as soon as you see the bridge. Portage on the right at river level to locate the track, then follow this past the swingbridge (make sure you check out the awesome gorge below it). Get back to the water at the first opportunity. Barrowman Flats are just below.

Barrowman Flat is a great put in for intermediate paddlers. From here to the take out is mostly class III+ with two or three class IV rapids that are easily portaged. Two schist gorges ensure that your scenery dollar is well spent. The second is one of the most spectacular on the Coast and makes the trip worthwhile on its own with some excellent play spots that will entertain experts as well. Take your little play boats, a good lunch and make a day of it. Low flows (40 cumecs) create a creek-like feel. At higher flows (above 90 cumecs) expect a fun, class III+ rollercoaster.

To get to the take out: find the Whataroa River bridge on SH6, turn eastwards on the gravel road on the southern side for 2km to the old bridge site. There is a large parking area, and camping is allowed. Make sure you have a ready stock of insect repellent because the sandflies are rather aggressive.

For post-river taste sensations head back to the Whataroa tea rooms and try some of Bills scones, or a Devonshire Tea, or a Bill's Bronco Burger. If you have had a really long day you might like to partake of all three!!

Where kayaking meets rock climbing—
Upper Crooked. (Richard Sage Collection)

WAIHO RIVER

The Waiho is a less intense excursion than the neighbouring Fox River just over the hill. This frigid stretch of water is rafted by companies based at Franz Josef and is a good section to try if you have never paddled the other ice-capades on offer. It certainly makes a good warm-up (??) for the Fox if you are unsure about your ability to handle intense cold and increased difficulty.

The rapids are fun in a weird sort of way—rafting companies must have the greatest marketing strategy in the world to entice people to pay to float down this icewater hydroslide. Mostly even gradient wave chains will roll you down from the put in to the bridge. Higher flows will see the same style of rapids, but much bigger and more confused water will ensure your frontal lobes won't thaw out for a week.

To get to the put in: simply drive to the end of the road providing access to the famous Franz Josef Glacier. Walk out to the river. The take out is at the bridge over the Waiho just out of Franz Josef township.

CLASS:	III+
LEVEL:	any
GAUGE:	visual
LENGTH:	4.5km
GRADIENT:	15m/km
TIME:	1.5-2 hours
PUT IN:	Franz Josef Glacier road end
TAKE OUT:	SH6 bridge over Waiho River
SHUTTLE:	4km
MAPS:	NZ Topo H35
CHARACTER:	freezing cold, even gradient
HOT TIP:	if the glacier keeps advancing the run will get shorter!

FOX RIVER

For those who like it on the rocks. The Fox River drains that which changes from a frozen state to liquid state. You guessed it: ICE straight from the famous Fox Glacier. The same stuff that forms the glacier floats down the river with you, explaining why that eddy you try for just keeps moving away.

CLASS:	IV+ (V-)
LEVEL:	most
GAUGE:	visual
LENGTH:	3km
GRADIENT:	23.5m/km
TIME:	1-2 hours
PUT IN:	from the glacier carpark or carry up to the terminal face of the glacier
TAKE OUT:	Fox River bridge SH6
SHUTTLE:	3.5km
MAPS:	NZ Topo G36
CHARACTER:	frigid, single channel, hard to read, somehow exciting water
HOT TIP:	you'll pray for one by the end!

The river starts off quietly from the glacier as class I-II riffles (with ice). Get your hands used to the cold so that you can deal with it lower down. Pogies are a good idea. The action picks up into class III-IV boulder gardens and quickly peaks after the swingbridge in a long narrow rapid with multiple drops and associated hydraulics. Scouting is prudent as there are places you don't want to be. The rest of the river is bouncy class III+ as the gradient eases right off just after the SH6 bridge and the take out. Photographers, or those who decide ice-yaking is not for them, can access the river via a track to the swingbridge just above the crux rapid.

Take this short run seriously. Even a capsize is potentially dangerous, water visibility is zero and it hurts to have any skin in the water. A swim would be very serious, so you should be paddling strongly at class IV level before even considering the Fox.

To get to the take out: from the Fox Glacier township drive south on SH6 to the Fox River bridge. The track up from the river is on the downstream, right side.

To get to the put in: follow signs to the Fox Glacier and carpark. Walk to your chosen put in spot.

Buller Westland
Section 7c

LANDSBOROUGH RIVER

One of New Zealand's most scenic and wildest rivers, the Landsborough flows from north to south along the Main Divide, linking Mount Cook and Westland National Parks with Mt Aspiring National Park. Seen from the river, which for the most part runs through tussock and beech flats, dense silver beech forest blankets rugged gullies and ridges as far as the snow line. Beyond, impressive ice cliffs and snowfields are spread over numerous snowcapped peaks.

The Landsborough was named by Julius von Haast for William Landsborough, a Scottish explorer who led expeditions into Australia. The Landsborough is known by Maori as Otoatahi—'the place of the toatahi' (male weka).

Flanked by mountains rising thousands of feet above the valley, the whitewater is challenging enough, given the Landsborough's remote and wild nature. At medium or low flows, most of the trip is class III or easier, with a handful of more difficult rapids, all portageable. As far as I know, the first kayak descent was by some competitors from the 1974 Commonwealth Games. Geoff Hunt and others pioneered the river for rafting from the early 1970s. The late 1970s saw a solo run by American Whit Deschner, described later in 'Does the Wet Suit You?'

The boundary of the Hooker-Landsborough Wilderness Area runs

CLASS:	IV (V)
LEVEL:	average about 1.4m (200 cumecs). Peak = 6.6m
GAUGE:	Haast River at Roaring Billy. Contact DOC at Haast 03 750 0809, or NIWA 03 768 0390 at Hokitika. Divide the flow in cumecs at Roaring Billy by two to get a Landsborough flow
LENGTH:	35km from Kea Flat
GRADIENT:	8m/km average, up to 14m/km in Upper Gates Gorge and above Kea Flat
TIME:	usually two days (but could be pushed in one)
PUT IN:	via helicopter to Kea Flat
TAKE OUT:	Clarke Bluff on SH6, at confluence with Haast River
SHUTTLE:	helicopter section 7C
MAPS:	NZ Topo G37, H37
CHARACTER:	remote, wilderness adventure, with stunning alpine scenery and cold water
HOT TIP:	one of New Zealand's best known multi-day trips

from McKerrow Creek, along the true right bank of the Landsborough, then up to the Solution Range opposite Barron Creek at the beginning of Toe Toe Flat. From Zora Creek the 'What The F**k Are We Doing Here' Gorge contains about six waterfall-type drops, all named by the first raft trip. From Hinds Flat down are several class III and IV rapids.

With access to the upper river restricted by the Hooker-Landsborough Wilderness Area, a good approach is to chopper from Clarke Bluff (Grid Reference G37 230864) and put down at Kea Flat, overnighting at Fraser Hut. From Kea Flat it's class II or III, with occasional surf spots and many straightforward chutes past boulder banks. Fraser Hut is barely maintained, so bivvy bags or tents are recommended. Be careful about camping in the wide open fields around Fraser Hut—the locals regard it as a landing strip for hunting parties...

Most of the whitewater action is within the Upper Gates Gorge. Things get interesting with Hunt's Hole, a class IV double-drop with a river-wide hole. This is followed by a long gentle left-hand curve with huge schist boulders at the bottom (The Squeeze, class IV), which can get very challenging in high flow. The crux at most flows is Hellfire, class IV+, a left turn with a series of rock sieves and a huge boulder midstream about three quarters down. A couple of class III rapids remain, including a hard right turn called Surprise Corner, before the river eases to Harper Flat and out to the Clarke. From the Clarke confluence near Strutt Bluff, it's about 45 minutes of flat paddling through braids to the Haast and SH6.

The amount of water dumped on this part of New Zealand is legendary. In flood, the Landsborough becomes monstrous and epics have occurred in the past. Getting in and out of the Landsborough valley by anything other than a helicopter is a major exercise, so parties should be well equipped and experienced. A favourable forecast is an absolute prerequisite, and packing a mountain radio is a sensible precaution. The regular high flows modify the riverbed, so always scout the major rapids.

Distances:
Clarke Bluff to Clarke confluence: 7km
Clarke confluence to Upper Gates Gorge: 14.5km
UGG to Fraser: 3km
Fraser to Kea Flat: 10.5km
Kea Flat to Hinds Flat: 7km
To get to the take out: drive east from Haast on SH6 to Clarke Bluff at

the confluence of the Landsborough and Haast rivers.

A useful campsite before the trip is at Pleasant Flat, about five kilometres south from Clarke Bluff on SH6. To avoid the flat paddle at the end, groups with 4WD or rentals may be able to negotiate a track from the bridge over the Haast river to near Strutt Bluff. The nearest pub is at Haast, where you can also visit the superb DOC visitor centre.

Jonathan Hunt

BURKE RIVER

"You've got to see this one," an excited Sean Waters babbled over the phone after the first descent of the Burke River with Jo Kippax, Richard Kersel and James McKeown in April 1996. Sean regaled me with stories: eight kilometres of continuous, steep, class V water that was mostly runnable—then a gorge, looked like V+ to VI for 1.5 kilometres, but they didn't run it. Caught by dark they spent an extra unplanned night out, but were convinced it was a classic trip. Proof that student loans are being spent on other things?

Here's Sean's description: the Burke River flows into the Haast River opposite the Burke Flats (on SH6 below the Gates of Haast). The run from the Monument (to a hunter who died up there years ago) is superb, continuous pool-drop paddling. The riverbed changes from huge boulders to a bedrock gorge, all of which is incredibly scenic. The Churn Rapids gorge near the end of the trip is 1.5km long and will challenge serious future hair boaters.

From the Monument to Cowan Creek the river flows in a mostly open valley with very steep (60m/km) bouldery rapids. Most are runnable, but rain would add some cushioning to the hard rock landings. If the river is very low, contemplate putting in around Cowan Creek. From this point the river runs into a gorge with excellent pool-drop paddling almost continuously to below the Hidden Rivulet confluence. About 200m below this, the river turns right in a tight, churning, bedrock rapid. It is a very good idea to get out here and scout the ensuing Churn Gorge. If you decide to walk, this is the last place to do it. Below, the river enters an incredible gorge up to 200m deep in places with some very big drops. From the safety of the gorge rim everything

CLASS:	V (P)
LEVEL:	needs a little rain for the top section and about 25-30 cumecs at the take out
GAUGE:	visual
LENGTH:	13.5km
GRADIENT:	35m/km (60m in the first kilometre)
TIME:	2 days
PUT IN:	the Monument at the head of the Burke
TAKE OUT:	Haast River confluence
SHUTTLE:	helicopter section 7C
MAPS:	NZ Topo G37, G38, E38
CHARACTER:	steep, tight, technical, super wilderness—no tracks, huts, nothin'
HOT TIP:	two days for 13.5km, who are you trying to kid?!!

looks possible, but there is no chance to portage or scout at all! We portaged the whole gorge on the left side using parts of an old tramping track and dropped back into the river via an abseil just past Raving Torrent Stream. This allowed us to run the last drops in this outrageous gorge.

To get to the take out: find Burke Flats on SH6 about 40km inland from the Haast township. Park in the gravel pits and leave room for the helicopter.

The put in is at the Monument in the upper Burke valley. If river levels are low, put in near Cowan Creek.

Sean Waters

Shit happens!! (Graham Charles)

TURNBULL RIVER

People used to talk in hushed tones about this jewel south of Haast. Catch some water on this run and you are in for some of the classiest class V moves in the country. It is off the beaten path, but is well worth the journey.

Horizon lines are the most common feature on the whole run, though everything is paddleable with a bit of thought and imagination. Wait for a little rain to bring out the river's full potential. At lower flows you can still get down, but some of the harder rapids may become portages when the bottom turns into rock landings with excellent pinning potential. Don't be misled by the distance. Allow a good couple of hours unless you know the run well.

Continuous class IV+ boulder gardens kick the trip off before a couple of larger drops make an entrance. The two crux rapids are about halfway. Both require a good deal of scouting and probably some soul searching as to what you're doing there. Both demand a definite, narrow line to finish after some testy manoeuvring and staying upright during the lead-in. Don't even contemplate turning over!! If you're prone to running rapids above your ability, a full-faced helmet may be your

CLASS:	IV+ (V)
LEVEL:	running clear after rain is optimal
GAUGE:	visual
LENGTH:	1.8km
GRADIENT:	39m/km
TIME:	2-3 hours
PUT IN:	top of the road at the Turnbull power station intake
TAKE OUT:	when the river flattens out (see text)
SHUTTLE:	2km
MAPS:	NZ Topo F37
CHARACTER:	steep, technical, boulder gardens
HOT TIP:	keep it a secret

saviour. The intensity eases slightly, except for a couple of class V drops. Suddenly it all stops. Continue to the first fork in the river, take the right fork. Right at the beginning look for a thinning in the bush. This is an old road. Take out and follow the road for 100m to an old river bed. Turn right and follow the river bed for 60m. Look for a cleared road on the left leading out to the main gravel road 800m below the power station.

To get to the put in: from Haast, head southeast 18km toward Jacksons Bay until the Turnbull River bridge. Cross and turn right to get to the farmhouse behind the camp ground. This is the home of Terry Eggeling. Collect the key from the house and arrange a time for it to be returned. Return across the river bridge and turn right onto a gravel road. Drive to the locked gate, carry on to the intake structure. There are plenty of sites for observers who can probably walk down the river bank faster than you can paddle with all the scouting and carry on.

To get to the take out: drive 800m down the main gravel road below the Turnbull Power Station.

The power of plastic. Jeff Sutherland on the Turnbull.
(Graham Charles)

WAIPARA RIVER

The Waipara was on the lips of every self-respecting adventure kayaker during the summer of 1995/96 shortly after its first descent by Sean Waters, Richard Kersel, Jo Kippax and James McKeown. They managed to 'shanghai' the helicopter pilot from Haast who wanted to put them in below the river's bottom gorge because he thought they'd never come out of there alive. Instead the team coaxed him into taking them up to the lake at the source of the river, and in doing so produced a classic river run. Sean picks up the description:

This isolated valley drains the Bonar glacier in Mt Aspiring National Park. The river takes you from the ice-filled névé lake out to the Tasman Sea (if you paddle the last section from the road bridge). The very long walk out if things go wrong and the sheer isolation provide a great sense of commitment and heighten the fun factor. The river is tight and technical at the top giving way to a series of sculptured gorges and pool-drop type rapids amongst stunning mountain scenery.

The Cabin Pass rapids leading out of the lake need a spring melt or a little rain water. These rapids are continuous class IV—tight and technical all the way down to the final bouldery rapid near Steward Creek. The action eases for a while before picking up in the Companion Ladder gorge. This contains an excellent series of class IV-V rapids that leads to Tar Pot Creek and a huge avalanche scar on the left side where we camped the first night.

Continuous class III boulder gardens start the next section with one steeper rapid near Butland Creek. The river enters a beautiful gorge just below Common Sailor Creek with a string of class IV rapids culminating

CLASS:	IV+ (V, P)
LEVEL:	requires a rain or spring melt—needs 10-15 cumecs at the put in
GAUGE:	visual
LENGTH:	20km
GRADIENT:	24m/km
TIME:	2-3 days
PUT IN:	source lake or below Cabin Pass rapids if there is not enough water
TAKE OUT:	Arawhata road bridge
SHUTTLE:	helicopter section 7C
MAPS:	NZ Topo E38, E39
CHARACTER:	steep, tight, technical, super wilderness—no tracks, huts, nothin'
HOT TIP:	when the going gets tough...

in the Saxton Drops just upstream of Cabin Boy Creek. We spent our second night near Campbell Creek.

Several kilometres of fun class III-IV water amidst huge boulders greet the new day before the river flattens out. It swings left and begins heading due west immediately before the bottom gorge. This begins with lots of class IV drops, some of which may have associated log jams. All are easily inspected and portaged if need be. A short flat section leads to a horizon line; take out on the left to portage. Huge boulder sieves lead down to an 8m waterfall onto big flat rocks. Below this the river eases slowly and you can choose where to get back in again. A few more rapids lead you to flat water flowing into the Arawhata River. From the confluence is a three hour float down to the road bridge.

To get to the take out: turn south off SH6 at Haast township and head towards Jackson Bay until the Arawhata River Bridge. It is best to leave your vehicle at the cattle yards on the north side and get picked up from there.

Sean Waters

Kiwis can fly. (Graham Charles)

WAIOTOTO RIVER

The Waiototo drains the Volta Glacier system on the western side of Mt Aspiring National Park. It is a beautiful river for intermediate paddlers wanting to get away for a wilderness self-support trip. The very idea of a Waiototo trip is to enjoy the wilderness experience, get a group of friends and enjoy it with some good food and wine.

Most trips start at the Bonar Flats. A short gorge between this point and the next flats—Donald Flats—contains a couple of drops in the class III range that add hydro interest to the scenery. The river is easy and becomes braided in the section down to the Drake River confluence.

The crux of the Waiototo whitewater comes in the next five or six kilometres to Ferny Flat. Most of the action is at the start of the gorge and is just into the class IV range, with portaging options if necessary. Once clear of the gorge proper the river widens into long, pleasant class II-III boulder gardens. There may be some boulder chokes in this section if the water level is very low.

Many parties spend the night on the Axius Flats at the Te Naihi River confluence.

From Axius Flats to the Palmer River confluence there's very little whitewater of significance except for a short rapid where the river narrows immediately below Caseys Flat. The scenery is superb and all you need do is float along with the current and contemplate life. The Palmer River confluence is the limit of jet boat travel up the Waiototo. From this point down to the bridge are easy shingle rapids.

To get to the take out: turn off SH6 at Haast and head south to the Waiototo road bridge.

CLASS:	III-(IV)
LEVEL:	most low flows up to high flows
GAUGE:	visual
LENGTH:	40km
GRADIENT:	4m/km
TIME:	2 -3 days (approx 12 hours of paddling)
PUT IN:	Bonar Flats
TAKE OUT:	Waiototo road bridge
SHUTTLE:	helicopter section 7C
MAP:	NZ Topo F38, F39
CHARACTER:	moderate wilderness trip, superb scenery
HOT TIP:	relax, take a break

CHAPTER EIGHT

CANTERBURY

Canterbury is a province of harsh contrast, its plains parched in summer by hot nor'westers, while winter brings snow, ice and a southerly surf. Across the plains braided shingle riverbeds chatter of their turbulent origins in hazy mountain ranges that hint of distant gorges and whitewater.

The proximity of good whitewater and a large population base at Christchurch has allowed the development of an energetic kayaking community in Canterbury. The Hurunui is a training ground for countless Canterbury paddlers before they progress to the Buller. It also has plenty to occupy the advanced paddler looking to sharpen skills, play in holes, rock splat their play boats, or pull wicked whirlpool moves. The Ashley, Opihi and Okuku are great get-away-from-it-all days when the water is there. The Rangitata Gorge still rates high in terms of challenge in the 1995 New Zealand Canoeing Association river survey—due mainly to the yarns generated by the strong Canterbury whitewater culture. The Waiau is an excellent weekend away and the Hooker—well, sort this one out yourself. And if all else fails, pray for a strong southerly and a six foot rolling surf at Sumner.

Canterbury's rivers guided Maori traders on their journeys to and from the pounamu fields on the West Coast. They would travel up the Whitcombe, Arahura, and Taramakau in the west and meet Canterbury's Rangitata, Rakaia and Hurunui. When their mission was completed, those rivers took them home again.

The Canterbury high country has been the realm of the farmer since the 1850s. Tough pioneers turned large tracts of land into something uniquely Kiwi and uniquely Canterbury. Stories, songs and yarns chronicle the understated hardiness of those who chose to live on remote stations such as Mesopotamia and Erewhon. The Canterbury high country and rivers were also visited by European explorers looking for easy transport routes to the West Coast.

Those resourceful pioneers and farmers also bred explorers of Canterbury's rivers and gorges. The history of first descents is largely undocumented. Many were explored decades ago by hunters and farmers on a variety of homemade contraptions. Most Canterbury rivers have, at the very least, been kayaked since the days of home-built canvas kayaks and canoes. Hugh Canard tells of trips into the Ashley in 1964 in homemade canvas canoes. I wasn't even born!!

The basement rock in the Canterbury mountains is predominantly greywacke, a moderately hard metamorphic rock which breaks easily along fracture planes—rather like Stone Age weetbix. Greywacke is easily snapped away by rivers, transported down country and deposited as round, tumbled river boulders, shingle or sand. Most Canterbury rivers have braided, gentle upland sections guarded by a final short gorge which provides the route to the plains. This geographical signature is obvious on the Rangitata, Hurunui, Ashley, Waiau, and Waimakariri.

The westerly airflow is the major player in the hydrodynamics of Canterbury. As an air mass crosses the Alps it cools, dropping its water vapour as rain. Most falls on the west side or just east of the main divide. Once rid of its water the air continues east as a warm dry mass. Eastern rivers depend on this weather pattern to fill them, as do their western cousins. It takes time for the water to reach the gorges because of the distance it has to travel. The water in the gorges rises and falls more slowly than in the mountains.

Canterbury rivers that do not have their headwaters near the main divide (Ashley, Okuku, Opihi) are different because westerly systems are rarely strong enough to push right across the country. Instead these rivers are filled by weather systems moving in from the south. Southerlies are far more common during the winter so rivers such as the Ashley are unlikely to flow through the middle of summer.

Once the westerly has deposited all of its rain on the divide it travels across the plains as a persistent, warm, dry wind (fohn) which drives the hardiest of souls to desperation. When this wind hits the constricted gorges of the upper river regions it speeds up. For anybody training or racing a slalom on the upper Hurunui this is maddening as you fly by yet another horizontal slalom gate.

Lowland Canterbury is in the rain shadow of the westerly system and gets very long, fine spells while the weather is reminding the sodden West Coast who is boss. Summer temperatures climb into the low thirties and leave paddlers gasping for some whitewater which inevitably becomes hard to find as summer moves on. Pray for rain or a frontal system to push some big surf into the Canterbury coastline.

There are plenty of other rivers in Canterbury to keep beginners and scenic cruisers happy. The Waimakariri offers a fantastic class II overnight trip (don't do it on the weekend of the Coast to Coast) in a lovely canyon. Put in at the Mt White bridge. The Rakaia River has 6km of class I-II water in its gorge. Further south the Pukaki and Tekapo have some good class III water when water is released into the channels (a list of release dates for the Pukaki is published at the start of the new year). The Rangitata has a good novice trip below the gorge down to the first road bridge. The lower Hurunui and Hope have pleasant class I-II conditions also.

Canterbury Rivers
Section 8

Boyle
Waiau
Lewis
Waiau
Hurunui
Okuku
Ashley
Waimakariri
Rakaia
Rangitata River
Hooker
Tekapo
Pukaki

WAIAU RIVER
GORGE RUN

It doesn't come much better. A multi-day package of interesting whitewater, great mountain scenery and fantastic camping makes the Waiau trip both rare and hard to turn down. One of the delightful features of this trip is excellent camping on flat grass sheltered by mature matagouri, surrounded by a plentiful manuka firewood supply. The trip can be done in two days, but considering the shuttle and the pleasurable camping many parties prefer three. Labour weekend, in October, is ideal as spring flows provide good water.

The trip begins one of two ways: a helicopter trip to just above the Henry River confluence, or a walk from Lake Tennyson over Maling Pass. The walk is along an open 4WD track and takes three to four hours depending on fitness and the efficiency of your carrying system. The first three hours paddling from the Henry River confluence involves a gentle float down a shallow stream —a chance to get used to a laden boat and absorb the views of Mounts Una and Faerie Queen in the surrounding Spenser Range.

Busy class III boulder gardens and narrowings between rock walls begin 1.5km below the Ada River confluence, near the Henry River confluence. About 2km from there, a lovely, long rapid known as Boulder Garden leaves many paddlers wishing for more. Unfortunately the river eases, but there are still many class III rapids to follow and

CLASS:	III-IV+
LEVEL:	needs spring run-off or a little rain
GAUGE:	visual, or Canterbury Regional Council flow phone 083 225 522 for the flow at Marble Point
LENGTH:	31km from Henry River, 45km from the Maling Pass put in
GRADIENT:	11m/km (from Henry River)
TIME:	2-4 days
PUT IN:	either via walking over Maling Pass or helicopter to Henry River
TAKE OUT:	at the first point on SH7 after the Hope confluence
SHUTTLE:	helicopter section 8 or 1.5 hours drive via Hanmer Springs to Lake Tennyson and the Maling Pass track
MAPS:	NZ Topo M31, M32
CHARACTER:	fantastic high country scenery, fun whitewater, a great weekend
HOT TIP:	don't swim in The Narrows

plenty of waves and holes to dally over if flows are good. The whole section is boat scoutable except one drop on a left hand bend after a short gorge. As the river opens out and flows under the McArthur swingbridge it signals 6km of class II spiced with the occasional good wave down to the Narrows.

The Narrows has a legendary reputation in excess of reality. The entry rapids have changed dramatically since 1995 and several drops have disappeared completely. The hazard is that if someone swims in the 1.5km long Narrows it is difficult to get out of the gorge. The main rapids are right at the start. At low flows a weir-like drop, appropriately named The Weir, requires a boof into the eddy on river right. At high flows this disappears and the entry is a churning mass of boils and buffers—a matter of keeping straight and paddling fast.

Arguments rage about the best portage route, if this is your choice. I say the best bet is to stay on the rocks on river right and seal launch back into the gorge after the rapids. Some hardy souls crash up to the road to Stonejug Hut, but that is a long haul.

After the Narrows the river is class II to II+ down to the Hope confluence. Many parties camp just below the Narrows (or use Stonejug Hut) and have a three or four hour trip out the following morning.

To get to the put in: either fly by helicopter or drive from Hanmer Springs to Lake Tennyson via Jacks Pass. At the top bridge over the Clarence River, a couple of kilometres from the lake, the track heads off on the western side of the bridge. Follow this up and over Maling Pass and down to the Waiau. Permission is required from the St James Station runholder Jim Stevenson whose phone number is in the Hanmer Springs directory.

To get to the take out: from the Hanmer Springs turnoff head west along SH7 for about 15km to Calf Creek. Find the small road which leads down towards the river and leave a car here. It is worth going down to the river as spotting the take out from the water without any prior knowledge is difficult.

Bruce Barnes

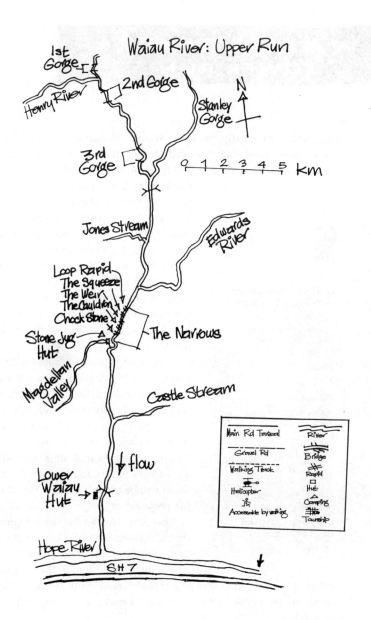

Waiau River: Upper Run

WAIAU RIVER
LOWER RUN

A classic beginner's trip, the lower Waiau's proximity to Christchurch, ease of access (and exits if needed), fun eddies and small rapids make it very popular with paddlers of all types of floating craft. We used to run Canterbury University Canoe Club trips to the Waiau with eighty or more budding kayakers, using buses as the preferred shuttle vehicle (which also kept the social side of these trips very sociable).

The first break out, requiring a ferry glide, is the trickiest piece of water on the river. The river pushes into a bluff which has flipped a significant number of novice kayakers. At least from here things can't get any worse.

Avoid bungy jumpers from the bridge as you float under it. For the first few kilometres the river flows through a shallow gorge. It opens out briefly then winds into a second gorge. Rapids are characterised by short sections of pressure waves with larger chunks of bedrock that might provide some grief for beginners. In higher flows the water will be more turbulent, especially in the gorge areas.

Immediately after the second gorge the river drops left around a large castle of rock in the middle of the river. This is known as the Sharks Fin—again, the cause of numerous nightmares for beginner paddlers. A couple of class I kilometres lead down to the bridge. Look out for and avoid willows on the last few corners.

To get to the put in: follow SH7 towards Hanmer Springs. Cross the Waiau Gorge Bridge and continue for a kilometre. Cross the Hanmer

CLASS:	II+ III
LEVEL:	class II+: < 150 cumecs class III: >150 cumecs
GAUGE:	Canterbury Regional Council flow phone 083 225 522 flow at Marble Point
LENGTH:	14km
GRADIENT:	4m/km
TIME:	2-3 hours
PUT IN:	above Waiau Gorge Bridge, river left
TAKE OUT:	Waiau River Bridge on Leslie Hills road
SHUTTLE:	16km
MAPS:	NZ Topo N32
CHARACTER:	single braid, moderate volume river
HOT TIP:	good squirting when the flow is up a bit

River and immediately turn down a gravel road on the left which heads towards the Waiau. Follow this to its end.

To get to the take out: head downriver on SH7 for about 15km to the Leslie Hills Rd turnoff. Follow this road 800m to the bridge across the Waiau.

HURUNUI RIVER

Flowing through an isolated subalpine valley, much of the attraction of the Hurunui lies in its easy, yet enjoyable rapids with excellent eddies for teaching and learning. It's Canterbury's most used beginner river, the first whitewater trip for countless neophyte Canterbury paddlers, site of many slaloms and training sessions, and a good hang out to escape the city scene. Take in and appreciate the grandeur of this remote valley while carving and turning your way down the river.

The slalom site at Jolliebrook has some nice surf waves, and the rest of the trip to Maori Gully is an eddy turning heaven, class II+. Try a squirt boat for lots of stern pivot action. The entrance to Maori Gully is obvious and there is a river access point on the upstream side of Seaward Stream. The river takes its overall class III/IV grade from Maori Gully.

Maori Gully has been a whitewater enthusiasts' haven since the 1970s and has seen descents by all manner of craft, including vehicles from the road high above! There are good play spots in the gorge depending on the flow. People have taken 2-3 hours to cover this 2km stretch. Pat Deavoll (first woman and second descent of Nevis Bluff) must win the perseverance award. Keen to improve her kayaking skills, Pat paddled Maori Gully 100 times in one summer! No mean feat.

CLASS:	III IV
LEVEL:	class III: <100 cumecs class IV: >100 cumecs
GAUGE:	Canterbury Regional Council flow phone 083 225 522, or *The Press* river information. Flow at Mandamus
LENGTH:	12.5km
GRADIENT:	5.6m/km
TIME:	1.5-5 hours
PUT IN:	Jolliebrook Swingbridge
TAKE OUT:	track at the bottom of Maori Gully
SHUTTLE:	(Jolliebrook-Below Maori Gully) 11km
MAP:	NZ Topo M33
CHARACTER:	even gradient, single braid, final 2km in bedrock gorge
HOT TIP:	for big excitement try mountain biking the shuttle with an umbrella!

Maori Gully owes its name to the people who once used the area as a route to the West Coast pounamu (greenstone) fields. From Kaiapoi they would travel through the Lake Sumner area, across the main divide and down the Taramakau River to the Arahura. They built flax and wood ladders to get into the side gullies entering the Hurunui gorge. The name

Maori Gully was given to one of the bigger side gullies, but has since become the name for the whole gorge.

Different put ins and take outs exist all along the run, which can be as long or short as you require, desire or before you expire. Camping is excellent and free at the Jolliebrook site or at the junction of the north and south branches. Use amenities where provided and remove all food scraps and litter.

To get to the river: drive to Waikari township (last petrol station and pub!) on SH7. Turn west and follow signs to Hawarden. Go straight through Hawarden, following signs to Lake Sumner Rd. The road turns gravel as you cross the Waitohi River and stays that way, climbing over Jacks Saddle and down to the Hurunui.

To get to the take out: the take out is near a clearing by a cattle stop where the road descends from Jacks Saddle and runs parallel with the river. At the end of this clearing is a track down to the river. If leaving a shuttle vehicle, drop it here.

To get to the put in: continue upriver over the south branch of the Hurunui to the Jolliebrook swingbridge and put in. There is a higher put in for the top gorge or 'fish farm' as it is known, but access can be a problem and permission must be sought from the farmer.

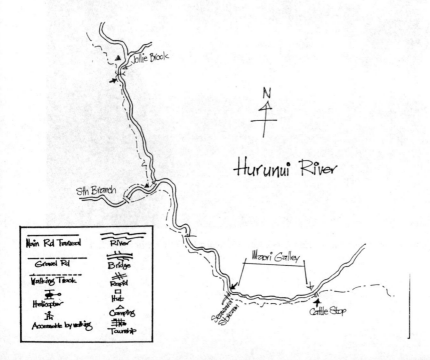

John Sanderson on the Marion Creek run, Hollyford River. (Graham Charles)

OKUKU RIVER

The Okuku is a tributary of the Ashley River west of Rangiora. A scenic, technical run, with several gorge rapids, the Okuku only flows in winter or during the August/September thaw. It is worth the effort in spite of the low temperatures and the need for a 4WD vehicle and shuttle driver.

Soon after the Okuku Pass Rd put in, a class III rapid gives a taste of what lies ahead. The next 8km is a mixture of class II and III rapids and play spots. The river flattens and widens. Watch out for a stock fence across the river acting as a strainer at high flows. It can be difficult to see. The remains of a similar stock fence are 1km downstream. After a hut on river right, the volume and gradient increases and the river enters a class III, tree-lined gorge. Watch out for trees in the river, especially after high winds or heavy snows. This section concludes with a large pour-over drop on a left-hand turn in the river.

The south branch joins in to produce a steep 7.4km stretch of class IV (V) rapids, dropping 13.5m/km. Depending on the flow a couple of drops may reach class IV+. They are worth scouting, as they are subject to change from flooding. The second of these is easily scouted or portaged on river right. The last few kilometres is continuous class III with several large holes. The river flow gauge appears on the river left and the road from Whiterock Downs is a little further down on the same side.

CLASS:	III-IV+
LEVEL:	20-60 cumecs
GAUGE:	Canterbury Regional Council flow phone 083 225 522. Ask for the flow at Whiterock Downs (generally a third of the flow of the Ashley)
LENGTH:	22km
GRADIENT:	12m/km
TIME:	4-6 hours
PUT IN:	Okuku Pass Rd ford on the Okuku River (via Okuku Pass or Lees Valley)
TAKE OUT:	Taaffees Glen Rd (off Loburn-White Rock Rd)
SHUTTLE:	37km (4WD track with fords)
MAPS:	NZ Topo L34
CHARACTER:	classic east coast gorge, technical pool-drop rapids
HOT TIP:	pull a sicky when the Okuku is flowing!

To get to the take out: follow the White Rock/Okuku Pass Rd from Loburn. Turn left into Taaffees Glen Rd. Obtain permission and the current state of the Okuku Pass road at the last farmhouse on the left at the end of this road. The take out is a further 1km on farmland where the road gets close to the river.

To get to the put in: return to road junction and head up the Okuku Pass road. Cross Okuku Pass and Lees Pass and descend to the Okuku River ford. The M34 map and a 4WD vehicle is the recommended recipe for success on this road! An alternative, but much longer route to the put in is the Lees Valley Rd on the west side of the Ashley Gorge.

Neil McKeegan

Whatever you do—remember to breathe! (Graham Charles)

ASHLEY RIVER

Canterbury paddlers are blessed with this little gem on their back doorstep. The Ashley has been kayaked, canoed, tubed and liloed for decades. It feels like a wilderness trip because of the depth of the gorge and anyone walking out faces a lengthy epic.

The Ashley was a pleasant sanity preserver during my university years. We used to skip lectures and head up for an afternoon paddle, especially when there was a good flow in the river. In summer flows it can be a little scratchy, but fine for people just breaking out of beginner stage. (Don't bother if flows get as low as three cumecs.)

For BIG action on the Ashley wait until a strong southerly front moves through and douses the catchment. Once flows pass 100 cumecs the fun really starts. I once got on the river at more than 200 cumecs, having crossed the snowfield at the put in wearing footwear and clothing appropriate to our student budgets (bare feet and sewn scrap garments). We told ourselves it was character building , in which case freezing southerly flood trips on the Ashley have accounted for a large proportion of my character.

On the river, settle in for the first few kilometres of easy paddling with lots of good eddies to warm up on. The crux of the paddling occurs about midway down the gorge in rapids that require manoeuvring to avoid the sharp, often shattered greywacke bedrock. About five rapids in quick succession create this crux section. One of them, a pour-over at lower flows, may require scouting by less experienced teams. Portaging is easy until levels are high enough to completely fill the riverbed, drowning any opportunities

CLASS:	III+ IV
LEVEL:	class III+: 4-120 cumecs class IV: >120 cumecs
GAUGE:	Canterbury Regional Council flow phone 083 225 522. Flow at the Gorge Bridge
LENGTH:	12.5km
GRADIENT:	7.5m/km
TIME:	2-5 hours
PUT IN:	Ashley River Bridge on the Lees Valley Rd
TAKE OUT:	Ashley Gorge campground
SHUTTLE:	about 15km
MAP:	NZ Topo L34
CHARACTER:	single channel, moderate gorge, small volume
HOT TIP:	Definition: character building—wait till there's snow on the ground, 200 cumecs in the river, a southerly wind, then go paddling

for scouting or portaging. Once past this section things ease off as the river winds its way down the final few kilometres to the campground.

If you venture out during floods don't take anyone without a proven big water roll. In flood the Ashley is cold and miserable, and a swim could turn serious. However the trip will fly—about 55 minutes is the fastest I've been down!

The campground warden offers a shuttle service for a fee. Call at the office if you want to make use of this.

To get to the take out: find the town of Oxford on SH72 about 40km west of Christchurch. From Oxford follow signs (which start in the town) to Ashley Gorge. The campground/picnic area is on the river right side of the bridge. Drive in to near the toilet block.

To get to the put in: head back towards Oxford. After a couple of kilometres you will see a sign to Lees Valley, Ashley Gorge. Follow this winding gravel road to the first road bridge over the Ashley river.

Teamwork is all important on the hard rivers. (Graham Charles)

OPIHI RIVER
GORGE RUN

It looks ominous, but the Opihi gorge run is an adventurous introduction to tight class III water with good eddy hopping. The initial 2km in the gorge is a class I-II warm-up to the first class III rapid. Scouting this rapid and the next is recommended as there are lots of willows to catch the unwary. Excellent class II+ rapids continue until the gorge walls open into farmland. Beware of fence posts in the river. There is an excellent play hole just before the bridge. Don't miss it.

To get to the take out: a few kilometres north of Timaru turn northwest onto SH8. Travelling west through Pleasant Point turn right at the Raincliff sign. Turn left immediately after Raincliff Camp. About 2km down this road veer left to Rockwood Bridge. Take out on river left.

To get to the put in: from the Rockwood Bridge hang a right up a metal road. Keep right at small intersections along the way. After 15-20kms turn right onto the main road to Fairlie. Look for the Opihi Gorge Rd on the right. Follow this to its end. It can be very boggy at times.

Wayne Johnson

CLASS:	III
LEVEL:	15-40 cumecs
GAUGE:	Christchurch Regional Council flow phone 083 225 522, flow at Rockwood
LENGTH:	10km
GRADIENT:	9m/km
TIME:	2.5-3 hours
PUT IN:	end of Opihi Gorge Rd, south of Fairlie
TAKE OUT:	Rockwood Bridge, Raincliff
SHUTTLE:	20km
MAPS:	NZ Topo J38
CHARACTER:	steepsided, technical gorge
HOT TIP:	something different

RANGITATA RIVER
GORGE RUN

The Rangitata Gorge, where water wages war on solid rock, is a legendary Canterbury test piece and adrenalin stimulant. A club could be formed from those who have paid penalty time in one of the bottom holes—perhaps called Rangitata Hydraulics Anonymous?

Like many Canterbury rivers the upper section meanders in braids as the river twists its way out of the Alps towards the sea. If there's no strong, persistent breezes up or down the valley then it's your lucky day (air pressure differences between the alps and the ocean are the engine that drives this annoying phenomenon).But unlike other Canterbury rivers, the Rangitata braids converge for a concerted attack on the last piece of greywacke bedrock that prevents the river from reaching the ocean in a relaxed manner. In this short, but intense gorge Glacier, Pencil Sharpener and Tsunami lead up to the first of the hard rapids—Rooster Tail, heralded by a good horizon line, prompts a scout from most teams. Below 70 cumecs the Pigs' Trough (hole at the bottom of Rooster Tail) is at its stickiest. The next rapid, The Pinch, has a number of named features but is essentially one rapid making up the main part of the gorge. It used to be the home of Harry's and Arlene's holes, but in 1995 a large chunk of bedrock collapsed into the river. Harry and Arlene were sent to hole heaven, leaving Hell's Gate in their place, considered to be a little less intense than its forebears. Shortly after is a tight constriction of boily

CLASS:	IV+ (V)
LEVEL:	40-350 cumecs. Harder at lower flows
GAUGE:	Canterbury Regional Council Flow Phone 083 225 522 or *The Press* river information
LENGTH:	10km
GRADIENT:	3.5m/km
TIME:	1.5-3 hours
PUT IN:	down track to river where road first returns to the river
TAKE OUT:	river right just above the spillway
SHUTTLE:	17km
MAP:	NZ Topo J36
CHARACTER:	even gradient, big water, short gorge
HOT TIP:	the home of Canterbury kayaking mega-gods/goddesses

water called The Slot, and that's about the end of it. After another kilometre, the gorge submits to the water and the river relaxes into more seemingly endless shingle braids to the sea. A road/track on river right indicates the take out.

This section of river has been rafted commercially since the late 1980s. Rangitata Rafts have their base on the road into the take out. They are very friendly towards kayakers and know the river better than anyone if you are after information on the river, flows and changes. They raft up to 200 cumecs. The river has been paddled at around 400 cumecs and provides a very fast, LARGE, ride with some interesting hydraulics. I would recommend this to very strong paddlers only.

To get to the take out: there are a range of options for getting lost on the back roads of south Canterbury. If you are new to the area and travelling from Christchurch get yourself to the small settlement of Hinds on SH1 south of Ashburton. From here follow the signs towards Arundel, Peel Forest. After 20km you will cross the Rangitata River bridge. Turn right immediately. The small settlement of Peel Forest is just over 30km from Hinds and has a service station and campground. From here follow signs to Rangitata Gorge. After 10km the road turns to gravel, a further 3km is a road junction with a sign to Rangitata Rafts. Take this road past the rafting base for about 4km to the river. Leave all gates as you find them.

To get to the put in: return to the junction with the Rangitata Rafts sign and turn right. Follow the gravel road 13km around the gorge. As the road starts to descend there is a gate and farm road on the right. Turn into this and after 200m you will be above the river.

HOOKER RIVER

The water is absolutely frigid and hard to read, you get an icecream headache if you turn over, and you're in big trouble if you swim! So why bother? Well, because there is something insanely fun about having to deal with these factors, and the paddling is excellent. On a more serious note if you are heading to Mt Cook make sure your vehicle is fuelled up before five o'clock.

The river responds to the mood of the glacier. If you go early in the morning when all the water is still locked up as ice in the glacier, expect a twisting, maze-like boulder garden. If the day is hot or a southerly storm is raging, you are in for a big, cold, scary rollercoaster ride. Watch out for moving eddies as large iceblocks float down the river with you.

We put into a maelstrom of ice and water during one of the frighteningly common southerly storms. Everything went fine until Greg Brosnan turned over. He rolled up in time to miss a big rock, but his boat hit it instead. Greg freaked, yelling he was sinking.

"Yeah sure Greg, it's just the cold water."

"No no, I'm sinking," he screamed as he paddled furiously to the bank. Sure enough he was getting low in the water. The bottom of his boat was cleanly punctured with a hole about 6cm in diameter. The plastic was so cold and brittle it snapped when he hit the rock. Be warned!!

To get to the put in: follow signs to the Hooker Valley from Mt Cook Village. Park at the end of the road and walk 900m to the first swingbridge in the Hooker Valley.

To get to the take out: follow the Tasman Valley signs to the road bridge over the Hooker River.

To get to the Tavern Bar for some good internal reheating: head back to Mt Cook Village.

CLASS:	IV
LEVEL:	any
GAUGE:	visual
LENGTH:	3.7km
GRADIENT:	16m/km
TIME:	1 hour
PUT IN:	first swingbridge Hooker Valley, 900m walk
TAKE OUT:	Hooker Bridge
SHUTTLE:	3.3km
MAP:	NZ Topo H36
CHARACTER:	even gradient, boulder gardens, glacial river
COLD TIP:	lads, this is what you will have!

CHAPTER NINE

OTAGO/SOUTHLAND

Opaline-coloured rivers tumbling through arid hills and mountains, searing dry summers followed by icy dry winters, local accents with a beautiful rolling rrr, plenty of stone fruit... a landscape that broke and was broken by humans in search of moa, gold, wool, mutton and electricity, and home to some the biggest big-water paddling in New Zealand.

Much of the history and culture of the region, fondly dubbed 'Central', revolves around the majestic Clutha River. New Zealand's largest volume river with a mean flow of 570 cumecs, the Clutha is the bearer of life to Central's parched (460mm of rain per annum) interior. In contrast to coastal Otago the inland plateau's extreme temperatures and devastating droughts correspond to its unforgiving landscape. But if the climate and landscape were harsh to humans, humans have been harsh back.

Otago's original moa hunting tribes set fire to thousands of hectares of forest in order to smoke out their prey. Fires raged up rivers, valleys and into the alps. Hills began to erode. By the time Europeans arrived there were few Otago Maori left—perhaps forced away by dwindling food and resources. From the 1840s graziers moving up the Clutha Basin brought fire and deforestation to an already delicately balanced, erosion-prone landscape. By 1860 Otago was grazing nearly 300,000 sheep on 112 runs. Winter ice worked its way into the faulted rock of an increasingly barren landscape.

A year later the Gabriels Gully Gold Rush on the Tuapeka (tributary of the Clutha) was the proverbial straw. Miners in their thousands picked and blasted the rock. The region's population quadrupled. Panning gave way to sluicing which led to dredging and vast tracts of earth were laid bare to the effects of erosion. The balance had been tipped. Soil washed into the rivers. Rain poured off naked hillsides unhindered by vegetation. The late 1800s saw a series of devastating floods with the biggest in 1878 which took an enormous toll on the residents of Central.

Last century's lust for gold may have carved today's Central Otago landscape, but this century's hydroelectric schemes have given the landscape new shape. Post World War II demand for electricity saw the Roxburgh dam placed smack in the middle of the Clutha River's length. New Zealand's great dam building era had begun. In 1992 the water rose behind the controversial and costly Clyde Dam, a disastrous legacy of the Muldoon Think Big era, which drowned the whitewater of the Cromwell Gap on the Clutha, and Sargood's Weir on the Kawarau River. The Clyde may not be the last—ECNZ is eyeing other sites on the Clutha for more dams. Look north at what is left of Otago's Waitaki River for a glimpse of Clutha-future.

Central Otago's rivers tumble among mica-schist boulders and riverworn gravel from catchments that reach back to snow and ice. They flow between massive walls of schists overlooked by barren hills—a landscape with a geological history of violent upheaval and gradual erosion. Schist is a metamorphic rock formed by the collision between the Pacific and Indo-Australian plates some 130 million years ago. Schist erodes into fine particles and thin plates, and fractures along planes within the rock creating the large overhanging slabs and sharp boulders characteristic of the Shotover and Nevis Rivers. Another characteristic of Central rivers is their blue-grey colouring which is caused by tiny grains of mica, one of many soft minerals within schist, eroded out by the constant action of water on rock.

The waters of the Kawarau drain the magnificent Lake Wakatipu. Fed by the Shotover, Arrow and Nevis rivers, the Kawarau has carved and sliced a 185km tract through some of the harshest country in New Zealand. Early travellers to Queenstown usually opted for the climb over the Crown Range, even in winter, rather than face the hostile rock canyon whose churning water was only crossable at the Natural Bridge near the Roaring Meg power station.

Paddling in Otago and Southland is as distinctive as the landscape. The Kawarau and Shotover command centre stage because of their mana, accessibility and commercial significance, while the sheer numbers of parochial Dunedinites ensures the Waipori and Taieri rivers earn their place in a national guide. The Manuherikia has become a popular 'harder' run since 1995 as the quality of this gorge became known to the wider community. The Nevis river is, and will remain one of *the* hardest, epic-generating runs in the country. The Mararoa, Grebe and Routeburn have fun water for those wanting to venture a little off the beaten path. And for those after more adventurous paddling, the Wilkin and Young rivers in Mount Aspiring National Park are places to go—don't forget your camera.

If you're looking for more in the region, try these rivers for moderate class II-III fun: the Eglinton out of Lake Gunn, the Waiau out of Lake Te Anau, and the Monowai and Mataura rivers. The Wairaurahiri drains Lake Hauroko into Foveaux Strait and is used as a fantastic class II paddling section in the annual Tuatapere Wild Challenge multisport race. The Mimihau, Catlins, Teviot and Pomahaka all have excellent water when in high flow. If further inland the Matukituki has a short rain-run, class IV section which requires some walking to get to. The Rees and Dart valleys have superb scenery and offer multi-day class I-II cruises by arranging transport to the top of these rivers via Wanaka-based jet boat companies.

Relaxed but aggressive on the Nevis River. (Peter Spiers)

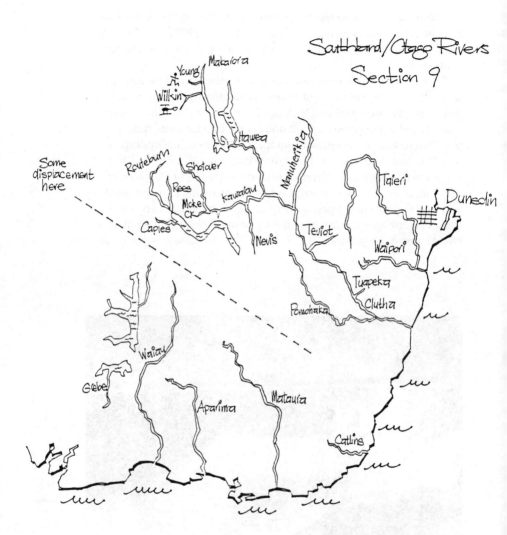

Southland/Otago Rivers
Section 9

YOUNG RIVER
MOUNT ASPIRING
NATIONAL PARK

The Waters/Kippax trip of Easter 1995 was an eventful one. They portaged up the Young River and have this to say:

The Young has a short, very scenic gorge between the Young Forks and Ram Flat near the Makarora. Below Ram Flat the river meanders easily out to the Makarora river. The gorge is relatively open with a track running close to the river on the left side.

Below the put in are several kilometres of pool-drop type rapids between boulders. These are reasonably continuous at around class III. Just above Ram Flat is the crux rapid, a 500m long class IV-IV+ rapid, Priopism, with a large drop near the top. This can be inspected from either bank and is visible from the walking track. Below this the river quickly eases to class I-II water down to the Makarora confluence.

To get to the put in: you can fly in by helicopter but the trip is short for the price you pay. The fun way? Is to float down a small side creek north of the township of Makarora to the Makarora River itself. Paddle across and carry for 2-3 hours up the Young track. The track offers good walking conditions.

When you arrive back at the Makarora, take out and carry your boat through farmland to SH6 then find your vehicle. This is adventure kayaking.   Sean Waters

CLASS:	IV+
LEVEL:	20 cumecs
GAUGE:	visual
LENGTH:	6.5 km
GRADIENT:	11.5m/km
TIME:	3 hours
PUT IN:	riverflats below Young Forks (2.5 hours walk)
TAKE OUT:	Makarora River
SHUTTLE:	walk or helicopter section 9
MAPS:	NZ Topo F38
CHARACTER:	steep, tight, technical
HOT TIP:	the walk will make you feel younger

WILKIN RIVER
MOUNT ASPIRING
NATIONAL PARK

The Wilkin provides a fine adventure in relatively civilised surroundings, and is another product of the Otago University First Descents Team of Sean Waters and Jo Kippax. While the lower reaches have been floated for years, this upper run was done for the first time during Easter 1995.

Between the upper airstrip and Kerin Forks hut is the main gorge which contains some beautiful technical boating amongst huge boulders. Below Kerin Forks is a pleasant float out to the Makarora and the main Haast Pass road. If very bumpy and steep paddling is the thing that makes your heart go pitter patter you may wish to check out the unpaddled section out of Lake Lucidus.

CLASS:	IV-V
LEVEL:	15-30 cumecs
GAUGE:	visual
LENGTH:	9.5 km to Kerin Forks 13.5 km to Makarora River
GRADIENT:	26m/km (to Kerin Forks)
TIME:	5-8 hours to Kerin Forks
PUT IN:	upper airstrip, Wilkin Valley
TAKE OUT:	Makarora River
SHUTTLE:	helicopter section 9
MAPS:	NZ Topo F38
CHARACTER:	steep, tight, technical
HOT TIP:	a fantastic part of the country with plenty of potential!

You can do the trip from the upper airstrip in a day, but relaxing in either, or both of the two huts is a nice option. The trip down the gorge can be combined with tramping parties and/or people who want to paddle the lower river (class I-II).

From the airstrip to the beginning of the gorge are some pleasant class II shingle braids. Once into the forest there is 200m of class III-IV boulder garden before the entire river sieves under a huge boulder. It's important to make the take out which comes up quite suddenly. Portage on river left. What follows are superb steep drops and chutes gradually easing to class III as you near Jumboland flat.

Below Jumboland, class III-IV paddling leads past a large slip on river right. This signals the beginning of the crux section, several kilometres of class IV-V boating. Somewhere in the middle is a nasty drop into an undercut wall which we portaged on the left. At the end of this section are some very hard drops and several tree sieves. We portaged 100m on river left to avoid these hazards. Once back on the water the paddling becomes progressively mellow down to Kerin Forks Hut. From here the river meanders over braided river flats to its confluence with the Makarora. After crossing the Makarora you end up on SH6 about five kilometres north of Makarora township.

To get to the take out: drive on SH6 between Wanaka and Haast to the small settlement of Makarora. The Wilkin river flows out adjacent to SH6 about five kilometres north of Makarora. A helicopter can pick you up in any clear area.

Sean Waters

In remembrance of Sargoods Weir. Killed by hydroelectricity. (Gordon Beadle)

KAWARAU RIVER
DOG LEG RUN

Triumphant surfing, enders, splatting, pivots and mystery moves at a variety of places, in a variety of flows on one of the biggest rivers in New Zealand. Summer flows may get as low as 100 cumecs, spring and flood flows may easily reach 600-700 cumecs. Whatever the flow there is always something to do.

After the put in the gorge closes in around you and an ominous roar heralds your arrival at the top of Smith's Falls. Find a wave, or if your life insurance policy is up-to-date catch a ride in the BIG hole on the right side. Beware of plummeting bungy jumpers off the second of the Twin Bridges. Violence may ensue if you try to get out on their platform unless it's a dire emergency. The best surfing on Do Little Do Nothing is during very high flows (greater than 400 cumecs) with a wave big enough for four. A long stretch of canyon with excellent pivot and ender spots leads into the final and crux rapid, Dog Leg.

Out of control surfing in the first part of Dog Leg is not to be missed—but often is as the waves are fast and difficult to catch. The final part of the rapid involves big confused waves that bounce down to the last 200m of flat water before the take out. You can go either side of the island. Getting out here is a good idea as Nevis Bluff lies just a few kilometres downstream and there are no more take outs.

CLASS:	III+ IV-
LEVEL:	class III+: 100-400 cumecs class IV-: >400 cumecs
GAUGE:	Otago Regional Council flow phone 03 479 6493, Chards Rd gauge
LENGTH:	7.5km
GRADIENT:	4m/km
TIME:	1-3 hours
PUT IN:	rafters' put in 4.5km from Arrowtown turnoff
TAKE OUT:	Dog Leg camping area
SHUTTLE:	6.5km
MAPS:	NZ Topo F41
CHARACTER:	big water playboating in a bedrock gorge
HOT TIP:	there is a UPW (ultimate play wave) at Do Little at about 450 cumecs

Camping at the take out is lovely, and there are some premium spots among the trees. At this stage it's free so let's look after it and keep it that way. If you plan to stay a while and use an open fire, please take your own firewood. After a decade of use people have pruned, cut and savaged the resident trees to a seriously depleted state.

To get to the put in: drive on SH6 between Queenstown and Cromwell. About 4km east of the Arrow River bridge is a gravel turning area with a road leading down to a carpark. A track leads to the river. Rafters clip their rafts onto a steep 'zip' wire. I know of kayakers who clip their boats onto the raft wire. I have also seen boats split from the impact at the bottom. Your choice.

To get to the take out: the take out is further along SH6 towards Cromwell, down the first turn left (gravel road) after the Gibbston Winery, or 150m after a sign to Coal Pit Rd. Drive down to the obvious camping/parking area. Be wary in rain storms. The steep hill to the parking area becomes very slippery and cars get stuck from time to time.

KAWARAU RIVER
NEVIS BLUFF

This run is the mountain pinnacle of whitewater kayaking in New Zealand. Nevis Bluff came into existence when the Kawarau river carved its way around a particularly tough piece of bedrock. As people moved through the area early in the twentieth century the road was established and the bluff had to be dealt with. Blasting and road cutting saw huge amounts of rock tossed into the river creating the rapids we know and love as Nevis Bluff.

The rapids have a chequered history: in 1980 a young paddler from Nelson, Chris Moody, attempted the rapids in an old fibreglass kayak. This attempt might have been successful had his trusty old boat not broken up around him. He apparently swam the rapids and finished up with the cockpit coaming hanging like a hula hoop around his waist.

In the 1981 *South Island Recreational River Survey*, Graham Eggar noted: "the rapids are unnavigable and exceedingly dangerous". Then in 1983, US kayaking guru Rob Lessor made an attempt. Having seen the rapid and heard the rumours, he was dressed in two life jackets as he pushed into the current. He did, however, put in below the first drop, thus eliminating the first two moves. The rest of his run was successful.

CLASS:	VI-
LEVEL:	90-300 cumecs
GAUGE:	Otago Regional Council flow phone 03 479 6439, Chards Rd gauge
LENGTH:	1km
GRADIENT:	25m/km
TIME:	60 seconds (to the bottom of the rapid)
PUT IN:	at the top of the rapid
TAKE OUT:	Victoria Bridge on SH6
SHUTTLE:	2km
MAPS:	NZ Topo F41
CHARACTER:	huge, huge, huge
HOT TIP:	try some reinforcing on your spray deck!

In July 1984 the gates at the Kawarau Falls bridge were closed for an assessment of the recreational, visual, and environmental impacts of hydroelectric development involving lowering the Kawarau's flow. The flow was reported to be 40 cumecs (lower than any recorded natural flow). Greg Bell and Gordon Raynor paddled the whole rapid and Tony Marcinowski put in after the first drops. It is interesting to note that these paddlers, talented as they were, had chosen to prepare for the run in the fashion popular at the time which was probably attributable to their success: *"Probably a kind of sixth sense telling me I was in a strange location bade me regain consciousness. A primeval survival instinct prevented me from yet opening my eyes. I was too frightened to move lest I disturbed the timpanist in my brain. My mouth felt like a small creature of the night had used it first as a latrine then as a mausoleum. Slowly, I opened my eyes; a big white thing stared down at me; I'd seen one before, but not from this angle. Over a bit further I spied a shower cabinet and some toothbrushes. Terrific—I had spent the night in the bathroom. Slowly, I arose and made my way to the lounge. I extricated my watch from a cup of cold tea—it was still early. The next thing I heard sounded very much like a bellowing hippo "C'mon—let's go pad-dling".....*" — NZ Canoe, Rafting magazine No.31, 1984

Through 1985, 1986, and 1987 many came and some went, but nobody could piece together the whole task. Terry Pairman and Rick McGregor, Stu Allan and Peter Kettering put in and paddled from below the first drop. Brian Parkes was immortalised on national television when he made an attempt, but got eaten in a rather large wave/hole and swam (underwater for some way).

The decade changed and Mick Hopkinson was in his fourth. He had been watching, dreaming and running this rapid in his mind since he first saw it. The flow was excellent (around 90 cumecs) and the rapid looked good (if you like that sort of thing). So, on August 24, 1990, Mick pushed off into the current and made the run in his characteristically clean, efficient style. Nevis had compromised.

A year later Pat Deavoll made the second and first female descent in a fibreglass slalom boat. This started a string of descents through the mid 1990s. Nevis has begun to relent, just slightly, but it has changed. It still remains in the realm of class VI. The summer of 1996 saw at least 10 descents at a range of levels, some as high as 300 cumecs.

For those who dare, or care, the put in is right above the rapid or you can paddle down the couple of kilometres of flat water from the bottom of the Dog Leg run. The take out is at the Victoria Bridge, 2.5km down-stream.

NEVIS RIVER

If you're into very steep, demanding creek boating and not afraid of an extreme physical and mental workout, this is your river. It's one of a kind. Nowhere else in New Zealand does a river drop this fast for so long, so only run this gem if you consider yourself an expert with nerves of steel and you're having a good week.

In 1985 Marcus Baillie and others made what is thought to be the first kayak descent of the river, although it had been run prior to this by Queenstown raft guides. Since then the river has been run by a number of teams with varying degrees of success. All the drops have been run but not on the same trip.

The river can be divided into three distinct sections. The first 2.5km are basically flat with the odd rock garden and ledge drop. At the end of this stretch is a delightful 2m pour-over (and a great photo opportunity). This is followed by a distinctive slot gorge about 1.5m wide and 20m long. Now the pace picks up. In the next 2km there are numerous drops up to 3m, and cascade rapids. Most require bank scouting and some you may choose to portage, although all the rapids in this section have been run.

The first 4.5km are the most delightful on the river. If you're not enjoying yourself here, a 4WD track on river left, 500m downstream of Potters Creek (river right) may be your last chance to exit with dignity.

The intensity of the river increases dramatically in a 5km combina-

CLASS:	IV-VI (P) V-VI (P) Make my day (P)
LEVEL:	class IV-VI (P): <10 cumecs class V-VI (P): 10-20 cumecs Make my day (P): >25 cumecs
GAUGE:	visual from SH6 opposite the confluence of the Nevis/Kawarau
GRADIENT:	25m/km average (59m/km through mid section)
TIME:	5-12 hours
PUT IN:	where the Garston-Bannockburn road meets the Nevis river at Nevis Crossing
TAKE OUT:	on the Kawarau river, 1.5km downstream of the Victoria Bridge
DISTANCE:	16.5km
SHUTTLE:	45km (includes 16.5km of gravel road)
MAPS:	NZ Topo F41, F42
CHARACTER:	very steep, tight, technical
HOT TIP:	take a sleeping bag and a couple of valium

tion of cascades, chutes and drops too numerous to mention individually, varying in height from 2m to 10m. The onslaught is relentless as the river plummets 220m in this open sided gorge. You'll probably find yourself paddling some, grovelling some and portaging lots in this section of the river, reminiscent of the Gates of Haast. Whatever you decide, be snappy about it, or you'll run out of time. One group of kayakers spent 10 hours in this section alone and bivvied overnight as a result (hence the hot tip). Portaging is easiest on river left, but you may need to cross the river and grovel on river right a couple of times. Take a throw bag too, some places require the use of a rope for the portage.

You'll know you've survived the middle section when you come to a runnable cascade rapid on a sweeping left-hand bend. From this point the intensity eases and the remaining 7km involves open style rock chutes. Before long Doolans Creek enters on river left and almost doubles the size of the river. Another kilometre and you'll hit the Kawarau. You'll never be so glad to see flat water.

To get to the put in: follow the signs from Cromwell to Bannockburn and from there the directions to the Nevis Valley/Crossing. You can camp at the Crossing, in the farmer's paddock by the bridge. This will help you get an early start on the river.

To get to the take out: the take out is on the Kawarau River a couple of kilometres downstream from the Victoria bridge (Citroen put in). Access to the Kawarau at this point is by a dirt track leading from the main road directly opposite the Nevis/Kawarau confluence. If you still want more action continue down through Citroen to the lower take out (see Citroen).

Ben Willems

KAWARAU RIVER
WAITIRI RUN/
CITROEN RAPIDS

Now the scene of much hooting and hollering as aspiring hardpeople cut their teeth on their first class IV+ big water, the Citroen, or Waitiri rapid, was hidden from the world for a number of years. "Easy flowing water," was how the *1981 South Island Recreational River Survey* described the section of river from Nevis Bluff to the Natural Bridge above the Roaring Meg run, obviously unaware of the existence of the rapid. It was not until about 1984 that a group floated down this stretch of "easy flowing water" to be confronted by Citroen. From then on it's been a classic and for years was the warm-up prior to a run down the now drowned Sargood's Weir (see Roaring Meg).

CLASS:	IV	IV+ to V
LEVEL:	class IV: < 300 cumecs class IV+ to V: >300 cumecs	
GAUGE:	Otago Regional Council flow phone 03 479 6493, Chards Rd gauge	
LENGTH:	3km	
GRADIENT:	10m/km (at the rapid)	
TIME:	1 hour	
PUT IN:	gravel road 2km east of Victoria Bridge	
TAKE OUT:	3km down the road at another gravel track to the river	
SHUTTLE:	3km	
MAPS:	NZ Topo F41	
CHARACTER:	one BIG class IV rapid	
HOT TIP:	a great first time, big water rapid	

Make no mistake, the water is big, but the moves are simpler than the heavy-weights of the big water world. There is a huge rock in the middle of the river which produces the crux move: brace right, brace left then line up and hold onto your hat for the run down to the big wave at the bottom. At high flows (>300 cumecs) the rapid turns VERY big and the rock forms a rather sizeable hydraulic that has forced swims from a number of the country's best big-water boaters. Even at normal flows I have seen very spectacular trashings in the bottom wave. Take a video camera and frighten your mother with the footage.

To get to the put in: this section is below Nevis Bluff. Drive on SH6 and look for a gate on the river side of the road about 2km east of the

Victoria Bridge (Nevis take out). Go through this gate and follow the gravel road a short distance down to the river.

To get to the take out: head downriver for about 3km. Just as the road starts to swing around a right hand curve there is a gravel road which cuts back down to the river. If you cross the Gentle Annie Stream bridge, you have gone too far. The rapid itself is way below a rock promontory 800m from the put in gate, a good viewing spot for shuttle drivers.

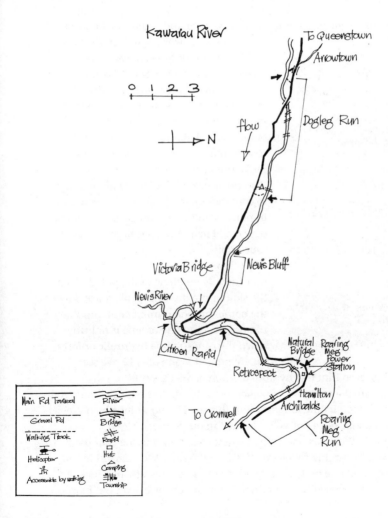

KAWARAU RIVER
ROARING MEG RUN

If boils and whirlies make your heart go pitter patter then get your teeth into this one. A fun run at any level with good surfing at regular intervals.

Once the scene of an annual battle of wire and string, the Roaring Meg slalom site was popular in the late 1980s, but has declined in use with dwindling numbers of South Island slalom racers. Attaching the wires to either side of the wide river was entertaining or frustrating, depending on whether you were observing or helping. The shattered gneiss rock through this region defies attempts to make things stay in it. How the engineers who constructed the Clyde Dam managed to convince anyone that a dam would stay in place is an interesting question. Maybe they could help build a slalom course or rodeo hole!

CLASS:	III III+
LEVEL:	class III: 100-350 cumecs class III+: >350 cumecs
GAUGE:	Otago Regional Council flow phone 03 479 6493, Chards Rd gauge
LENGTH:	5km
GRADIENT:	5m/km
TIME:	13 hours
PUT IN:	carpark 800m upstream of the Roaring Meg Power Station
TAKE OUT:	the secret roadside area 5.2 km along the road
SHUTTLE:	4.5km
MAPS:	NZ Topo F41
CHARACTER:	big water boils and swirlies, narrow bedrock canyon
HOT TIP:	squirty heaven

At flows around 150 cumecs there is a user friendly playhole at the put in. After the slalom site the whirlpools spiral down the gorge through a number of unnamed rapids. The only one of note is halfway down the run—a large hydraulic unfortunately named Man Eater. I have seen proof, however, that this hydraulic is non gender specific.

From here down enjoy the scenery and the endless seams to bury your tail in. Take some time to reflect that this slackening water which now runs into a lake once flowed on to the famous Sargood's Weir.

Sargood's Weir was one of the biggest, best rapids in the country. There were not many solid class V BIG rapids (200-500 cumecs) in the world. We had one of them. It exuded power, technicality and lack of emotion. Paradoxically it demanded of its suitors awe, fear, but most of all respect. It remained unpaddled until 1980 when Mick Hopkinson, then on holiday from the UK, paddling a fibreglass slalom boat successfully ran the rapids. Rob Lessor from the USA claimed the second descent in 1983. Then in 1984 Mick Hopkinson with partner in crime, Dirk Passchier, returned again. Dirk claimed the first 'Kiwi' descent of Sargood's. Through the late 1980s it became 'the rapid' for any aspiring hardperson and saw a number of descents. The intensity of use increased when the plans were published which showed that the lake from the Clyde Dam was going to flood the area to immediately above Sargood's Weir. People were keen to paddle the rapid before it died. When it finally drowned a slow and lingering death in 1992, Mick, who had paddled the rapid eighteen times, mourned its passing like a lost friend—indeed it was. May this murder of an international resource never be allowed to happen again.

To get to the put in: find the Roaring Meg Power Station on SH6. the put in is 800m towards Queenstown down a gravel road which descends a short distance to a large gravel carpark. A track leads to a gap in the gorge walls and the short clamber down to the river.

To get to the take out: from the power station drive about 4.5km down SH6 to a gravel road on the right cutting back down to a gravel parking area. There are some grey road marker posts numbered along this side of the road. The road is just after the 39 marker. If it is your first time on the run go down to the river so you can identify the exit point when you get there.

SHOTOVER RIVER
MACLEOD'S TO SKIPPERS RUN

If it was anywhere else with easy access this class II+ section of the 'Shotty' would be one of the most used runs in the country. As it is the road adds a little spice to a day in the upper valley. Try to avoid rainy days as the road gets very slippery. Many have been stuck.

The great thing about this run are the numerous ledge-type reversals that provide excellent play spots for those wanting to sharpen their retentive moves or just learn to sit in a hole. The river is deep in the gorge and has a strong wilderness feel until you reach the Skippers Canyon Bridge and are bombarded by falling bungy jumpers.

If considering the section from Skippers Bridge to Deep Creek (class I), it is worth contacting the jet boat drivers at the Skippers Bridge. The drivers are in radio contact with each other and will let everyone know there are kayakers on the lower section. This will save the fright and possible trauma of meeting a high speed craft unawares.

Camping is great at the MacLeod's put in area. Stay the weekend and mix the kayaking with the superb mountain biking further up the valley.

CLASS:	II+
LEVEL:	any
GAUGE:	visual
LENGTH:	7.5km
GRADIENT:	4m/km
TIME:	1.5-4 hours
PUT IN:	MacLeod's Bluff
TAKE OUT:	Skippers Bridge boat ramp
SHUTTLE:	8.5km
MAPS:	NZ Topo F40, F41, E41
CHARACTER:	scenic canyon, fun play holes and eddies
HOT TIP:	don't drive off the road

To get to the take out: drive up to Deep Creek, (see Shotover Gorge run) continue for about 6.5km to the Skippers Canyon Bridge. Drive down to the river level downstream of the bridge. Park, but leave room for the trucks and buses that turn around at the river.

To get to the put in: from the Skippers Bridge area drive nearly 9km of narrow winding road to a short dirt road on the left which leads into an area of willow trees.

Shotover River

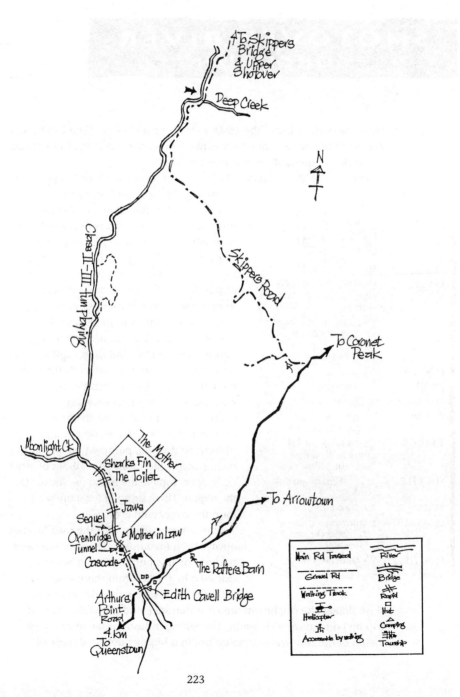

To Skippers
Bridge
& Upper
Shotover

Deep Creek

N

Skippers Road

To Coronet
Peak

Class III–II tunnelling

Moonlight Ck

The Mother

Sharks Fin
The Toilet

Jaws

Sequel

Oxenbridge
Tunnel

Cascade

Mother in Law

To Arrowtown

The Rafters Barn

Arthurs
Point
Road

Edith Cavell Bridge

4 km
To
Queenstown

Main Rd Tarsealed	River
Gravel Rd	Bridge
Walking Track	Rapid
Helicopter	Hut
Accessible by walking	Camping
	Township

SHOTOVER RIVER
GORGE RUN

From the gold rushes of the 1860s to the tourism boom of the 1990s, New Zealand's richest river has been exploited for over a century. Signs of this are apparent along the whole journey.

The late 1800s saw gold fever hit the Shotover region, or Molyneux as it was then known. Much early river diversion and tunnel digging was done at this time. Legends abound of the hardy souls who toiled through freezing winters waist deep in the frigid water searching for the elusive strike. Temperatures get so cold that in the winter there are some 'seeps' from the walls that have been visited by ice climbing enthusiasts from Queenstown.

Gold is still being extracted ounce by ounce from the river, but most capital returns comes from the surface of the river these days. The Queenstown tourism machine works the river's scenery, whitewater and history mostly through rafting and jet boating. Horse riding, historic sightseeing, parapenting, mountain biking, scenic flights and a plethora of other activities complete the menu for visitors to the region. These bring in far more gold than the river could ever yield.

Human interaction with the river has not always been favourable. The river has been treated harshly, but in return it has extracted a high price from those who bed with it. Miners were regularly caught by flash floods (the catchment area is unforested, and rainwater runs off rapidly) and never seen again. The rafting industry is the most recent victim of the Shotover's exploitation. In a highly publicised spate of

CLASS:	IV	IV+ to V
LEVEL:	class IV: 30-60 cumecs class IV+ to V: 60-90 cumecs	
GAUGE:	visual at the take out, or Otago Regional Council flow phone 03 479 6493	
LENGTH:	12.5km	
GRADIENT:	13.5m/km	
TIME:	3-5 hours	
PUT IN:	Deep Creek on the Skippers Canyon Rd	
TAKE OUT:	Oxenbridge Tunnel above Edith Cavell Bridge at Arthur's Point	
SHUTTLE:	16km (9km rough dirt road)	
MAPS:	NZ Topo E41	
CHARACTER:	scenic canyon, single channel, technical whitewater	
HOT TIP:	it's gotta be done	

incidents several tourists have drowned while participating in commercial rafting trips and the consequent loss of confidence in rafting has hurt the Queenstown economy.

The main gorge carves through outcrops of schist, while fine mica gives the river its silty colour. This stuff is gritty, gets through everything and is hard on wearers of contact lenses. The water is very cold, even in summer, so it's wise to wear a winter set of gear on this river. Don't be put off.

After waving 'auf wiedersehn', or 'sayonara', to the rafters at the Deep Creek put in, the water is class II for most of the gorge with good play holes and awesome scenery.

The action is in the final 1.5km at a section of rapids called The Mother, which doesn't announce itself in an obvious way. Watch for a narrowing in the gorge, the disappearing horizon line and a rock that looks like a shark's fin, aptly named Shark's Fin. Scouting throughout The Mother is easiest on the left. The Toilet is next, scene of many a good flushing. For many it is the crux rapid, requiring a dodgem move between the two lead-in holes and a good line into the Toilet. Jaws and Sequel take you down to Hobson's Choice: the Oxenbridge Tunnel—or Mother-in-Law.

The Oxenbridge Tunnel was chiselled, cut and blasted from solid rock by the Oxenbridge brothers in an attempt to redirect the river and expose whatever treasures may have lain in the riverbed. It was an idea that didn't work but paddlers now must contend with the brothers' legacy. Paddle into the black hole in the cliff. If you can't fit, the river is too high! (If this is your first time on the river ask the rafters if they are running the tunnel.) Once inside, aim for the white blob of light and brace on the right. Water boils up from the right wall and tends to push you into the undercut left wall. Keep your boat pointed straight. People have broached in this tunnel and swum out without their boats. Always keep in the back of your mind that the light at the end of the tunnel might be an oncoming train!!

Upon exiting the tunnel you're on the runway to the Cascade, another artificial rapid. The only stipulation on this one is to stay upright. The rocks below water are sharp and will slice you and your gear very nicely.

The Mother-in-law option follows the natural bed of the river to the left of the tunnel. It has a sharp drop at the top that pushes hard into rocks downstream. Once clear of this drop it is all over.

Spare a thought for the original Ironman competitors in the late 1980s who paddled light fibreglass downriver racers down the entire river.

To get to the take out from Queenstown: head to Arthur's Point via Gorge Rd. Immediately before crossing the Edith Cavell bridge turn left onto a gravel road. Follow this for 600m to the bottom of Cascade rapid.

To get the put in: head back across the bridge. Continue east for a couple of kilometres to the junction signposted: Coronet Peak, Skippers Canyon. Turn left and climb for 4km. Turn left at the next sign to Skippers Canyon. Turn left again onto the gravel road. This road is very rough and windy. Rental cars are not insured on this road—bad luck. After 9.5km of slow driving, allowing rafting vehicles to pass whenever they want, you will arrive at the Deep Creek put in.

Kayakers have been known to get caught out by snap freezes in Skippers Canyon, Shotover River. (Dave Vass)

GREBE RIVER

CLASS:	II-III+	**TAKE OUT:**	end of the road at Lake Manapouri
LEVEL:	above 18 cumecs		
GAUGE:	visual	**SHUTTLE:**	3km
LENGTH:	3km	**MAPS:**	NZ Topo D42
GRADIENT:	11m/km	**CHARACTER:**	easy boulder gardens, beautiful scenery
TIME:	1 hour		
PUT IN:	Percy Valley Bridge, Grebe Valley, Fiordland National Park	**HOT TIP:**	take a mountain bike and get dropped at Borland Saddle

You have to work for this one. It is a long way off the beaten track and best suits those in the area for other reasons (tramping, mountain biking). The run is moderate and needs water to make it worthwhile. Locals say it gets to class IV in very high flows. Maybe it does, but you can decide.

To get to the put in: head to the deep south and Borland Lodge, west of Monowai and north of Lake Monowai. Drive past the Lodge and through the gate on the road over the Borland Saddle. Follow this winding gravel road for 37km to the Percy Valley Bridge.

To get to the take out: continue 3km down the road to the south arm of Lake Manapouri where there is a DOC public shelter and toilets. Take plenty of HEAVY DUTY insect repellent!!

MARAROA RIVER

The Mararoa flows from the two Mavora lakes between Lake Te Anau and Lake Wakatipu and empties into the Waiau River. It is a beautiful area and the river trip no less. Camping at the lakes is stunning and I suggest taking mountain bikes for exploring further up the valley.

From the put in at the lake it's a fantastic float alongside honeydew beech forest and through clear pools where trout cruise beneath underwater ledges. The forest gives way to a short gorge as the rapids pick up, climaxing with three drops. Rumour has it these can get to class IV in very high flows, but at anything other than a big flood they are class III. The rapids settle as the gorge eases and the river breaks into farmland down to the next short gorge under the Kiwi Burn swingbridge. This small section is used often for beginner teaching sessions and novice slalom races. Take out and walk up the track to the carpark.

To get to the put in: turn off SH93 (between Lumsden and Te Anau) at signs to Mavora Lakes. Twenty six kilometres of gravel road takes you to the lakes and camping areas. Park near the first swingbridge and put in.

To get to the take out: drive about 5.5km down the valley and look for a DOC sign on the left side, opposite a gate, indicating access to the Kiwi Burn area via a swingbridge. Head down a farm track for 800m to the parking area near the bridge.

CLASS:	II-III
LEVEL:	above average flows
GAUGE:	visual, and *Southland Times* fishing levels, anything more than low and clear
LENGTH:	6.5km
GRADIENT:	8m/km
TIME:	1-2 hours
PUT IN:	the first swingbridge at South Mavora Lakes
TAKE OUT:	the Kiwi Burn swingbridge
SHUTTLE:	5.5km
MAPS:	NZ Topo E42, D43
CHARACTER:	scenic, single braid, small gorges
HOT TIP:	go for the weekend, take your mountain bike

ROUTEBURN RIVER

This short but exciting stretch of the Routeburn descends beside the popular walking track of the same name. It is a small river, and in normal flows more of a rock crash than a kayaking trip. However the river becomes a viable option when rain falls.

The run is tight and technical from the start. After the first kilometre a steep section drops 20m in 500m. Scouting for logs trapped amongst the boulders will be necessary, which detracts a little from the run, but the paddling is fun and the surrounding forest and scenery adds to the trip.

To get to the take out: follow the Glenorchy-Routeburn road from the small settlement of Glenorchy. Cross the Dart River and turn right onto the Routeburn-Kinloch road to a parking area and track to Lake Sylvan.

To get to the put in: continue up this road to the top carpark and put in by the swingbridge.

CLASS:	IV-V
LEVEL:	needs extra water
GAUGE:	visual
LENGTH:	4km
GRADIENT:	22m/km
TIME:	1-3 hours
PUT IN:	swingbridge at the top carpark on the Routeburn-Kinloch Road
TAKE OUT:	next footbridge down
SHUTTLE:	3.5km
MAPS:	NZ Topo E40
CHARACTER:	tight, technical, some trees
HOT TIP:	take a wood saw

MANUHERIKIA RIVER
OPHIR GORGE

Rapidly gaining the status as one of *the* runs to do in the area, the Manuherikia has been popular with Otago paddlers since its first descent in 1988. A small, tight gorge, it needs more than normal flow, but thanks to the Otago flow phone system you won't have to waste time driving to the river to check it out.

Initially the gorge is narrow and water flat. The rapids begin after 3km. A diversion tunnel on the right after 5km heralds the beginning of the gorge proper. Between the beginning and end of the tailrace are a number of steep technical class III-IV rapids. All are easily portaged on the tailrace. They continue 2km past the tailrace outflow. Two steep and technical class V rapids follow each other in quick succession, both with high objective danger from rock sieves and undercuts. Flows above 1.2 gauge fill these rapids in, but the water becomes very turbulent and confused and stays class V. Below, the gorge relents before issuing onto Central Otago farmland just after the Chatto Creek confluence. From here to Keddell Rd is a half hour of flat water. It is possible to take out at Chatto Creek and walk 4km along the old railway line to the Chatto Creek pub.

CLASS:	IV (V)	V
LEVEL:	0.5-1.3	1.3-1.5
GAUGE:	Otago Regional Council flow phone 03 479 6493	
LENGTH:	12km (to Chatto Creek confluence)	
GRADIENT:	10m/km	
TIME:	4-6 hours	
PUT IN:	Ophir Bridge below Omakau	
TAKE OUT:	end of Keddell Rd	
SHUTTLE:	15km	
MAPS:	NZ Topo G41, G42	
CHARACTER:	scenic canyon, technical, tight rapids	
HOT TIP:	some of the easiest portages in the country	

To get to the put in: 1.5km east of the small settlement of Omakau on SH85 is a short gravel road down to the Ophir bridge. Put in there.

To get to the take out: drive east on SH85 towards Springvale. Look for Keddell Rd. Turn down this and follow it 1.5km down to the river.

TAIERI RIVER
UPPER GORGE

The Upper Taieri Gorge is a renowned tourist attraction and is followed for much of its length by the line used by the Taieri Gorge Excursion Train. It flows through a strikingly barren landscape between high schist cliffs. The run is very flow dependent. Often only paddleable in the winter after southerly rain, the Taieri is nonetheless one of the finest whitewater trips close to Dunedin and worth doing if the opportunity arises.

The usual start for the trip is off Pukerangi Rd where the road and the railway share a single bridge over Sutton Stream. Easy rapids for 6km lead down to the Castle Hill or Pump House Rapid, class III-IV depending on the flow. More continuous rapids follow, but gradually ease for a few kilometres. A large triangular boulder warns Hole in the Wall is approaching. This is a straightforward 2m drop, but it should be inspected from the right. At high flows it is possible to run a ramp on the left, but the usual route is more central.

Boxcar Rapid, now clear of the railway boxcars that used to form an additional hazard, lies below the Deep Stream confluence. This class IV rapid is the hardest on the trip. Big waves feed into stoppers at the top and a diagonal strainer wall at the bottom. After one more rapid the river eases to the take out upstream of the bridge at Hindon.

To get to the put in from Dunedin: drive via Mosgiel to Outram on SH87 and on towards Middlemarch. About 50km from Outram (and

CLASS:	III-IV
LEVEL:	20-90 cumecs
GAUGE:	Otago Regional Council flow phone 03 479 6493
LENGTH:	27km
GRADIENT:	5m/km
TIME:	4-6 hours
PUT IN:	off Pukerangi Road at the Sutton Stream confluence
TAKE OUT:	Hindon railway station
SHUTTLE:	allow an hour from take out to the put in
MAPS:	NZ Topo H43, I43, I44, J44
CHARACTER:	a medium volume river with sections of continuous whitewater and shorter rapids formed by schist boulders
HOT TIP:	watch out for scarfies!

about 7km before Middlemarch), turn right onto Pukerangi Rd and drive about 3.5km to the road-rail bridge over the Sutton Stream. Cross the railway line and carry 100m down to the river.

To get to the take out: the take out is across the river from the Hindon Railway Station (signposted from the George King Memorial Drive—take a good map!). Cross the bridge and drive a few hundred metres upstream to a gravel beach, river left.

Rick McGregor

Classic Kiwi Shuttles #4. (Paul Chaplow)

TAIERI RIVER
LOWER GORGE

Otago University's answer to stress management, the lower Taieri gorge trip is good whitewater within half an hour of Dunedin.

The run begins at the Mullocky Stream confluence after 20 minutes walk down a private track off the Mt Allan road from Taioma. Easy water for 1.5km leads to the class III-IV Pipeline Rapid just downstream of the pipeline from which it takes its name. At higher flows, a rapid called Trinity (from its series of three holes) forms on a left bend about 700m below Pipeline. Rock Garden is 1.5km from Trinity beneath a prominent bluff on the left and a right bend. Run the first section on the left, then work across to the right for the second half. There are easier rapids at Bum Rock (a split rock which one can paddle through at suitable flows) and at Lee Stream. A flat paddle of several kilometres leads to the take out on the left at Outram bridge.

A flow between 45 and 100 cumecs at Outram makes for a good class III+ to IV trip, though it is also possible at lower and higher flows.

To get to the put in from Dunedin: take SH87 from Mosgiel towards Outram for about 4.5km. Turn right on Tirohanga Rd, then left after 3km onto Taioma Rd. The road climbs steeply, then descends into Mullocky Stream after about 6km. A short distance up the other side of the valley, a road (not marked on the map) turns left at a locked gate. Portage about 1.5km down this road (under the railway viaduct) to the river. To get to the take out: return to SH87 and continue for about 5km to the Outram Bridge.

CLASS:	III-IV
LEVEL:	25-100 cumecs
GAUGE:	Otago Regional Council flow phone 03 479 6493. Flow at Outram Bridge, greater than 104.5 optimal
LENGTH:	10km
GRADIENT:	12m/km
TIME:	2-3 hours
PUT IN:	off Taioma Road at the Mullocky Stream confluence
TAKE OUT:	Outram Bridge
SHUTTLE:	14km
MAPS:	NZ Topo I44, J44
CHARACTER:	a medium volume river with several good rapids formed by schist boulders
HOT TIP:	watch out for 'hair scarfies'

Rick McGregor

WAIPORI. RIVER

The Waipori River drains Lake Mahinerangi and flows down through a series of dams to join the Taieri River on the Taieri Plains near Dunedin. When water is released in the upper stretches of the river, it creates steep, technical water in an attractive gorge surrounded by native bush. For the trip to be possible, the hydro company has to be spilling water from its Number 3 Dam. Ring the Control Desk at Waipori Falls (Dunedin Electricity).

The river can be easily split into three different sections or run together, whatever you want, or are capable of.

The first section begins below the Number 3 Dam, near Waipori Falls village with 500m of class III-III+ rapids. The river then eases to class II and III. Two Douglas fir trees on the left bank herald the approach to a short class III+ to IV rapid, where the river divides round a rock island. The left is the usual channel. Take out if you want at the Number 3 Power Station below a two-arch bridge after about 3km. To continue, paddle down the lake for 1.5km to the Number 4 Dam, which is portaged on the right.

The second and crux section starts below Number 4 Dam. A side road leads down to the dam through a locked gate. The technical paddling begins about 500m into the section with a rapid containing boulder chokes and probably logs. The next hard rapid, marked by a small side stream on the left, has two drops in quick succession, with a powerful hydraulic at the bottom of each. There are a couple more class IV rapids before the take out at the Number 4 Power Station.

The present generation regime for the Waipori power stations provides

Sections 1, 2   Section 3

CLASS:	III-IV (1st section) IV-V (2nd section) II (3rd section)
LEVEL:	20 cumecs
GAUGE:	Otago Regional Council flow phone 03 479 6493
LENGTH:	7km
GRADIENT:	14m/km
TIME:	3-4 hours
PUT IN:	below Waipori Number 3 Dam
TAKE OUT:	at Number 4 Power Station
SHUTTLE:	7km
MAPS:	NZ Topo H44
CHARACTER:	perhaps the most 'North Island' of the South Island rivers, tight and technical
HOT TIP:	be careful of trees in the river

about 20 cumecs downstream of the Number 4 Station more often than in the past, but none in the upper river. Contact the Generation Manager at Dunedin Electricity for up-to-date information.

The third and lower section is a pleasant beginner's trip of mostly class II with one short class III rapid, The Cascade. Take out at the road bridge.

To get to the take out from Dunedin: drive south along SH1 to the Taieri River bridge. Continue for about 4km and turn right on the Henley-Berwick Road. From Berwick (about 5km), follow signs towards Waipori Falls. A gravel road leads up the valley, initially on the true left and then on the true right. The road begins to climb away from the river after about 9km at the Number 4 Power Station.

To get to the put in: continue for about 7km, past the Number 3 Station to the Number 2A Station and Number 3 Dam, just near the entrance to the Waipori Falls village. Park outside the Number 2A Station, carry down to the left of the powerhouse, and put in on the true right below the Number 3 Dam (about 400m down from the power-house).

Rick McGregor

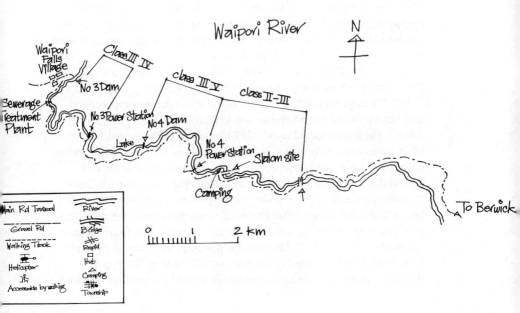

CHAPTER TEN

FIORDLAND: MILFORD SOUND AREA

Wilderness doesn't get much wilder, isolation more complete or rivers as steep as they do in Fiordland National Park, New Zealand's first World Heritage Park. Fiordland is the home of the Milford Track, Homer Tunnel, Darran Mountains, sandflies, and of course, some excellent kayaking. This vast and remote park (1.2 million ha) is guarded in the west by a forbidding coastline, and bounded in the east by a string of lakes and three major rivers—the Hollyford, Eglinton and Waiau. Of these the main kayaking interest centres on the Hollyford, along with a number of other smaller rivers in the Milford area accessed from Te Anau along the Milford Road (SH94).

This rugged, cold part of the country held little appeal for early Maori who settled only as far as Martins Bay (see Tutoko River description). According to legend, goddess of the underworld, Hine-nui-te-po, released sandflies throughout Fiordland to stop people from lingering, captivated by the work of the god Tu-te-Rakiwhanoa, who had carved the incredible landscape. The Hollyford Valley was used as a greenstone trading route that linked the West Coast at Martins Bay with Otago.

In 1770 Captain James Cook sailing on the *Endeavour* approached and named Dusky Sound, the largest of Fiordland's fiords, but did not enter it. His second expedition in 1773 surveyed Dusky Sound, but little other exploration inland was done by Europeans until the 1860s—dense bush, towering mountains, incredible amounts of rain and general inaccessibility turned most away. But in 1863 the miner Patrick Caples travelled up the Routeburn Valley, crossed Harris Saddle and descended into a large river valley (which he named the Hollyford) then made his way to Martins Bay to become the first European to cross from Otago to the West Coast. In 1889, W.H.Homer reported to the Wakatipu County Council that he had found a new pass to Milford from the Upper Hollyford. Homer claimed that this saddle could be tunnelled, although

236

it would be 51 years before his prophecy was proven. Work began on the tunnel in 1935, with the breakthrough made five years later that opened the way to Milford Sound and the forests, mountains and rivers of Fiordland.

Driving into the upper Hollyford, through Homer Tunnel and down the Cleddau Valley to Milford Sound, you'll find it difficult to comprehend the age of the rocks and the forces that created the park's stupendous glacier-worn valleys and peaks. Five hundred million years ago, when much of New Zealand lay under the sea, immense pressure and heat hardened sediment into the crystalline granites, quartzite, serpentine, marble and banded gneisses that are found in Fiordland today. These rocks were folded, faulted and pushed up from the ocean. Then, around the time of the first insects, volcanoes strewed lava flows across the surface, while diorite and gabbro formed from molten rock. During the period when dinosaurs walked the earth, Fiordland sank beneath the sea for about 65 million years. When it was pushed to the surface once more, the land was split by great faults and sharply uplifted to form huge mountains. In the past two million years glaciers have worn away the mountains, forming the steepwalled U-shaped valleys seen today, many of which were flooded by the sea to create fiords.

River catchments in the Milford area are relatively small and dry up quickly. The saving grace for paddlers is that Fiordland is one of the wettest places on earth. With an annual coastal rainfall up to seven metres, the rivers don't dry up often. When it rains, it rains hard and it's generally not worth thinking about paddling anyway. Most beat a path to the tavern at Milford Sound. As with the West Coast's rivers, catching things on the drop is the best bet.

The kayaking in the area is generally difficult—most runs involve negotiating boulder gardens, and steep ones at that. The Marian Creek Run on the Hollyford, and the Arthur River are the pick of all for quality. Gunns Camp and Falls Creek runs, also on the Hollyford, and the lower Cleddau, offer more moderate water for intermediates. The upper stretches of the Hollyford and Cleddau rivers, and the lower Tutoko, will tempt 'hair boaters' when the water levels are right.

There are plenty of good camping places. One of the nicest would have to be in the Homer Hut area just east of the tunnel. Gunns Camp in the Hollyford Valley, and Milford Lodge in the lower Cleddau, both offer accommodation. Milford Lodge has a shop, showers and washing facilities. Petrol and diesel are available at Milford Sound, but don't expect anything after 5pm.

To date there has been no control put on any of the rivers in the Milford region. Most hydro efforts have been to the east on the big lakes. Let's hope it stays that way.

HOLLYFORD RIVER
MONKEY CREEK–
FALLS CREEK

Steep and gnarly best describes the upper run on the Hollyford. This one needs rain, and lots of it. It will be possible only when the Marian Creek section is far too high to contemplate. The gradient looks impressive, but be aware the first kilometre is flat before the river drops at over 50m/km!

Most of the action is well within the class V league. If you are not totally solid on this sort of water don't even bother getting your boat off the car. The portages are in the first third of the trip where the river moves away from the road. Scouting is necessary for much of the journey. It is possible to bash back to the road at any stage if conditions get too bad (or good!). The gradient eases just before Falls Creek, but at the flows necessary for this run the water stays pushy right to the Marian Creek swingbridge.

To get to the put in: Monkey Creek flows into the gentle upper valley area just below Homer Hut. The creek is signposted on the bridge crossing it. Make your way down the creek to the river.

To get to the take out: Falls Creek take out is on SH94 1km west of the Hollyford Valley turnoff. Marian Creek swingbridge is 1km down the Hollyford from the turnoff.

CLASS:	V+ (P)
LEVEL:	enough water to get down it
GAUGE:	visual
LENGTH:	7km
GRADIENT:	40m/km
TIME:	3-5 hours
PUT IN:	Monkey Creek (off SH94 just below Homer Hut)
TAKE OUT:	Falls Creek
SHUTTLE:	7.5km
MAPS:	NZ Topo D41
CHARACTER:	very steep, tight and technical. A serious proposition
HOT TIP:	whoa, hooo, haaa, waaa!

HOLLYFORD RIVER
FALLS CREEK TO MARION
SWINGBRIDGE

A great 'in-between' section for those just pushing into class IV paddling. Easier than the two hard Hollyford runs, but more difficult than the Gunn's Camp run. The overall difficulty depends very much on the water level. If the water is high after rain or snow-melt expect a class IV trip. If the water is low you will crash down predominantly class III rock filters with a couple of individual class IV drops. One of these may need to be portaged at any level. The whole run can be scouted and seen from the road.

To get to the put in: find the Falls Creek bridge on the Milford road 1.5km upstream of the Hollyford Valley turnoff.

To get to the take out: drive down the valley to the Hollyford Valley turnoff. Turn off and drive 1km on the gravel road to the carpark at the Marion Creek swingbridge.

CLASS:	III-IV
LEVEL:	running clean
GAUGE:	visual
LENGTH:	2.5km
GRADIENT:	28m/km
TIME:	1-2 hours
PUT IN:	Falls Creek
TAKE OUT:	Marian Creek swingbridge
SHUTTLE:	2.5km
MAPS:	NZ Topo D41
CHARACTER:	tight, technical, miniature boulder gardens and steep chutes
HOT TIP:	a good warm-up for the next section

HOLLYFORD RIVER
MARION CREEK RUN

The stuff of dreams and fantasies...water crystal clear in the shallows and deep green in the pools, rapids like a chess game—steep, challenging, requiring a variety of complex precision moves. All this against the scenery and backdrop of the northern Darran Mountains. No wonder paddlers from all over the world rate this stretch of class V water the best in New Zealand. Whatever your preferences there is no doubt that this is a top class section and the fact that it is roadside (or close to it) adds to its attraction. Most parties who visit the area will do multiple runs on this stretch. It is very good.

A gentle warm-up for 1.5km leads to the first and longest gorge with more than a dozen solid class IV+ to V rapids. If you can find someone who knows the river you will knock hours off your trip time. The rapids are hard to boat scout as large granite boulders and steepness restrict visual inspection to small sections at a time. If in doubt—scout. The gorge traps lots of wood which shifts regularly. This run has seen its fair share of pinnings and entrapments through poor route choice or just plain stupidity.

A short easy stretch after the first gorge allows time to relax and enjoy the scenery. Two short gorges follow. The first has a mandatory portage at the start. Be very wary because the lead-in is easy, but the take out eddy is not built for more than two at a time. Check out the size of the logs perched upon the large boulders and imagine the flood that put them there!

CLASS:	IV-V (P)
LEVEL:	running clean and looking low in the first section
GAUGE:	visual
LENGTH:	8km
GRADIENT:	32m/km
TIME:	3-5 hours
PUT IN:	Marion Creek swingbridge
TAKE OUT:	Gunn's Camp (check with the camp manager that it is okay to exit via the camp)
SHUTTLE:	7km
MAPS:	NZ Topo D41, D40
CHARACTER:	steep, tight, technical
HOT TIP:	the closest thing in New Zealand to roadside hair boating. Many people rate this *the* premier trip in NZ

The last gorge has a portage at the end around a rapid which ranks in the 'make my day' class. Portage on either side of this class VII prospect which I'm sure will be run one day by someone very skilled and lucky, or by someone unlucky who missed the take out eddy. The falls into the pool at the top of the rapid are possible and are run a few times each season. Don't miss the break out! The water at the top pushes surprisingly hard *away* from the eddy. Back on the water, float the remaining kilometre to Gunn's Camp. When the river splits, take the right-hand channel which puts you outside the camp.

To get to the put in: turn off the Milford Road (SH94) at the obvious sign to Hollyford Valley. Drive 1km on the gravel road to the carpark at the Marian Creek swingbridge.

To get to the take out: continue down 7km of gravel road to the small collection of huts at Gunn's Camp. Ask the camp manager for permission to park and use the area to exit the river.

HOLLYFORD RIVER
GUNN'S CAMP RUN

Crystal clear class III water against the beautiful northern Darran Mountains makes this a great day out for intermediate paddlers. Keep an eye out for logs come to rest after being washed down from the upper sections in high water. Ask for permission from the campground owner before getting on the water.

The Moraine Creek rapid is a 500m-long class IV boulder garden at the end of the run. It drops 20m through this length and is fun if you want to add some more excitement to your Milford journeys.

To get to the put in: from the Milford Road turn off to the Hollyford Valley. Drive about 7km of gravel road to Gunn's Camp.

To get to the take out: continue along the road for about 8km to the Moraine Creek rapid, visible from the road. Park at the top or bottom of the rapid depending on where you want to get out.

CLASS:	II-III+ (IV)
LEVEL:	running clean
GAUGE:	visual
LENGTH:	8km
GRADIENT:	12m/km
TIME:	2-4 hours
PUT IN:	Gunn's Camp (check with the manager if accessing the river through the camp)
TAKE OUT:	on the Hollyford Road where it joins the river 8km from the camp, or Moraine Creek swingbridge
SHUTTLE:	8km
MAPS:	NZ Topo D40
CHARACTER:	scenic, moderate boulder gardens and straight-shot rapids
HOT TIP:	a great trip for strong intermediate paddlers

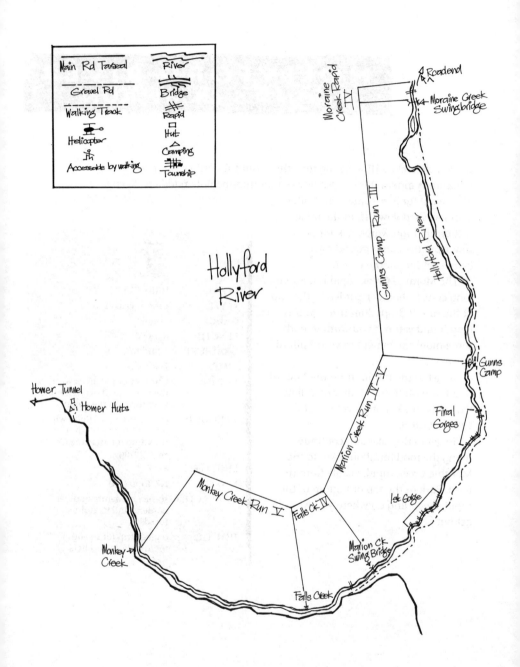

Main Rd Tarseal

Gravel Rd

Walking Track

Helicopter

Accessable by walking

River

Bridge

Rapid

Hut

Camping

Township

Hollyford
River

Moraine Creek Rapid IV

Roadend

Moraine Creek Swingbridge

Gunns Camp Run III

Hollyford River

Gunns Camp

Homer Tunnel

Homer Huts

Marion Creek Run IV–V

Final Gorges

1st Gorge

Monkey Creek Run V

Falls Ck IV

Marion Ck Swing Bridge

Monkey Creek

Falls Creek

CLEDDAU RIVER

"A great run," Sean Waters told me before my first trip to the Cleddau. "From The Chasm," he added. It didn't feel like kayaking to me. We scratched and crashed down with more walking and grovelling than anything else. I came away disgruntled and called Sean to question the legitimacy of his parents. He was adamant that with some water, the vital ingredient we were lacking, it was a great run. So here it is.

Wait for rain, preferably quite a lot of it if you plan to run from The Chasm. It starts steep and the rapids are reminiscent of the Marian Creek run on the Hollyford. Not long after starting is one very steep, as yet unrun rapid, best portaged along the road. Back on the river the gradient remains steep all the way to the Donne confluence. Everything else has been paddled, **in the right water**.

At the Donne the gradient eases and class IV water lasts for a kilometre or so, then it's into class III and II before Milford Lodge.

To get to the put in: go through the Homer Tunnel, drive down the Cleddau Valley to The Chasm carpark, pose for pictures among the hundreds of tourists. Scramble out the end of the carpark down to the river. If you're getting in at the Donne River, either bash down the Donne river itself for 150m, or drive 500m further towards Milford from the Donne River bridge where the river runs close to the road.

To get to the take out: drive down the valley and turn off at the signs to Milford Lodge. The Lodge is a backpacker hostel with camping sites, a shop, showers and washing facilities if you need these. (There aren't any others in the area.)

CLASS:	IV-V+ (P), or IV from the Donne River
LEVEL:	running high
GAUGE:	visual
LENGTH:	2.5km (Chasm-Donne), 5km (Donne-Milford Lodge)
GRADIENT:	40m/km (Chasm-Donne), 12m/km (Donne-Milford Lodge)
TIME:	2-5 hours
PUT IN:	The Chasm carpark or the Donne River confluence
TAKE OUT:	Milford Lodge
SHUTTLE:	8km
MAPS:	NZ Topo D40
CHARACTER:	steep, tight, technical
HOT TIP:	take sturdy shoes

TUTOKO RIVER

Dr James Hector, a geologist for the Otago Provincial Government, bestowed the name Tutoko on this stunning mountain and river valley during his explorations in 1863. Tutoko and his family lived at a small pa in Martins Bay at the time Hector was attempting to find a pass out of the Milford area. Hector had explored the upper Cleddau region only to be *"repelled by the wall of mountains"* so he sailed to the Hollyford to follow in the tracks of other explorers back towards Central Otago.

The Tutoko is a great boulder garden run when the water is right. The main thing is to check the water level at the bridge before heading up the valley. The top rapids are the hardest. Take note of the time and the gradient. Most teams have taken a long time to run the top kilometre. There are some portages, plenty of scouting to do and the action is continuous.

To get to the put in: drive to the Tutoko River bridge. Parking is better river left of the bridge, but the track starts on the right. Follow the track until you feel like getting on the river, or until you reach the open river flats, or until you collapse with fatigue and can go no further. It's amazing that kayakers have such skinny legs!

To get to the take out: paddle down the river!

CLASS:	IV-V (P)
LEVEL:	running clean and manageable at the bottom, but needs some extra water in it
GAUGE:	visual
LENGTH:	4km
GRADIENT:	40m/km
TIME:	6-8 hours
PUT IN:	Tutoko River Flats
TAKE OUT:	Tutoko River Bridge
SHUTTLE:	walk—sorry, but it is good for you
MAPS:	NZ Topo D40
CHARACTER:	steep, tight, technical with Mt Tutoko as a fantastic backdrop
HOT TIP:	take the same shoes as the Cleddau

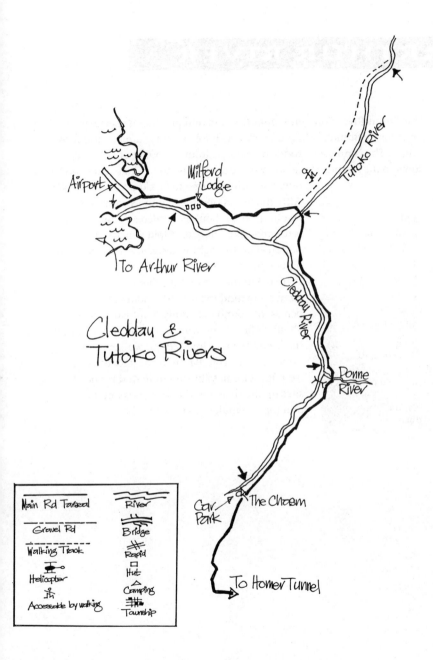

Airport

Milford Lodge

Tutoko River

To Arthur River

Cleddau River

Cleddau &
Tutoko Rivers

Donne
River

Car
Park The Chasm

Main Rd Tarseal

Gravel Rd

Walking Track

Helicopter

Accessible by walking

River

Bridge

Rapid

Hut

Camping

Township

To Homer Tunnel

ARTHUR RIVER

The Arthur River flows into Milford Sound and provides a spectacular route for the famous Milford Track which follows it for almost its entire length. The commonly paddled section is from the outlet of Lake Ada down to the Sound. There are two channels leaving the lake. Take the left one. Parts are reported to be class V in big floods. After the first island the channels converge, creating class II boulder gardens. At the next fork is another more difficult rapid which can be portaged on the right if necessary. This leads into a pool and the final rapids.

To get to the put in: take the road to the wharves behind the airport. Paddle directly across the sound to Sandfly Point Hut and jetty. Shoulder boats and wander up the valley. Forgive the amusement of any Milford walkers who happen to see you. Put in at the jetty at Lake Ada. It is also possible to put in at a range of sites up the river, but the walk in is not difficult and the run makes up for it.

CLASS:	III-IV+
LEVEL:	needs water
GAUGE:	visual
LENGTH:	4km
GRADIENT:	10m/km
TIME:	2-3 hours
PUT IN:	Lake Ada
TAKE OUT:	Milford Sound
SHUTTLE:	walk
MAPS:	NZ Topo D40
CHARACTER:	super scenic, fun whitewater
HOT TIP:	make sure your car has plenty of fuel

GLOSSARY

Boof: method of landing the kayak flat after clearing a nasty drop. 'Boof' is the onomatopoeia for the sweet noise the boat makes when successfully completing one. Not recommended on very high waterfalls unless you wish to become vertically challenged.

Cartwheel: rodeo move in which the kayak flips nose and tail in quick succession to create a vertical 360 degree turn. Good move.

Carving: a wide radius turn using the force of the water to turn the boat.

Crux: the critical, crucial, most important or serious bit of a rapid, river or problem.

Down River Race: a whitewater race from one point to another, the fastest person wins. Has its own specialist type of boats hence Down River Racer.

Down time: the time you spend stuck in, under, or anywhere else in a hydraulic.

Eddy: Bruce Barnes' dog? Or more commonly the recirculation of water in behind rocks, walls and other river features.

Ender: when the water pushes the nose or tail down so the boat stands vertically.

Eskimo roll: Otago wintertime river snack (see roll). Or a method of righting a capsized kayak while still in it.

Green room: the quiet place below the whitewater you visit doing serious down time when swimming.

Hair boating: paddling at the limit of the grading system (because it makes your hair stand on end with fright).

Hareboating: paddling nowhere near the limit of the grading system but your hair stands on end with fright anyway.

Hole: a recirculating hydraulic that can hold a kayak and its occupant for controlled or semi-controlled fun, or out-of-control horror, depending on the size of it.

Hydraulic: a water feature caused by some irregularity in the riverbed which causes the water to recirculate in the vertical plane. These form on a continuum from waves-holes-weirs.

Intense: where people often sleep. Otherwise describes a particularly hard, continuous section of river with no rests.

Loop: an ender which carries on over.

Move: any manoeuvre(s) which can be passed off as intentional.

Mystery Move: using the force of the water to push the whole kayak beneath the water surface—when and where you resurface becomes a mystery to you and your buddies.

NIWA: National Institute of Water and Atmospheric Research.

Penalty: what a kayaker pays for making a mistake. Measured in pain, downtime, beer or Drambuie, depending on the circumstances.

Pinning: water trapping a kayak where it doesn't want to be (between rocks, trees, bridge supports). Can be a very dangerous situation if the kayaker can't get out.

Pirouette: pivoting the boat vertically, nose down, from an ender.

Pivot: by using the force of the water a kayaker sinks the tail of a kayak making a fast turn or pivot. Done vertically it's also known as a whoopee or stern squirt.

Piton: the result of crashing nose first into rocks. Usually over vertical drops. The result of not boofing.

Play: a concept that is thrashed out of us prepuberty by paranoid grown-ups. An attempt to re-find an important developmental medium. Essentially doing something for no reason other than fun. Play boat: a small volume kayak designed mainly to play in holes and waves.

Play spot: a place for playing.

Poodles: silly looking, useless dogs which do tricks, but they're just not real dogs.

Portage: character building exercise of taking one's boat for a walk (leashes optional) to get to a river or to miss a rapid you don't want to paddle.

Pour-over: a smooth flow of water over a rock or drop.

Retendo: half a cartwheel, landing you back in the hole.

Rock splat: like it sounds. Splatting your boat vertically against a rock or bluff via a pivot or stern squirt and using water pressure to keep it there. A recreational version of pinning.

Rock sieve: A section of river where the water sieves between rocks and offers no navigable route for a kayak.

Rodeo: freestyle kayaking competition in which kayakers get points for controlled (?) moves in a play spot. Out-of-control penalty time will score points as well. Strange sport.

Roll: bread filled up with yummy stuff which gets wet and squashed if it's yours, looks great if it's someone else's, and gets left behind when you're really hungry. See also Eskimo roll.

Seal launch: method of getting to the water from on rocks, banks, cliffs etc. Climb onto the kayak and slide into the water.

Shuttle bloke or bunny: a term of reverence for those lovely people who drive vehicles from the put in to the take out and wait, swatting sandflies, for the next four hours with or without complaint—we love you all.

Slalom: a competition in which a strange sect of kayakers race down a rapid through a series of poles (gates), as if the sport isn't hard enough already! The idea is to get to finish as fast as possible without touching any poles, which actively try to hit you.

Squirting: see Pivot. Can also be a urinary tract or bowel reaction when inspecting difficult rapids.

Surfing: good delaying tactic at the top of a big rapid. Find a wave to play on and let someone else go first.

There-I-woz: mandatory opening phrase to any epic paddling story.

Trashing: a loose term for being outa control at the mercy of a hole, evoking anything from hilarity to extreme horror depending on the severity.

Weir: a smooth flow of water over a uniform ledge. Most commonly human-made and potentially lethal as water recirculates evenly from a long way downstream.

Wiper: rodeo again—a tail-first retendo combined with a roll. Looks hard but isn't. A good face-saving move.

APPENDICES

HELICOPTER OPERATORS

Section 2

Heli Sika
Poronui Station
RD3, Taupo
Phone: 07 384 2816
Type of machine: Hughes 500d, 500c
Ideal loads: 2 or more
Method of carry: sling load
Range: Upper Mohaka, Ngaruroro

Section 5

Amalgamated Helicopters
Duncan Sutherland
Carterton
Phone: 06 379 8600
Fax: 06 379 8759
Mobile: 025 428 790
Type of machine: Hughes 300d
Ideal loads: multiples of four
Method of carry: slingload
Range: Waiohine, Otaki

Section 7A

Tony Ibbotson
Last Resort
Box 31, Karamea
Phone: 03 782 6617
Fax: 03 782 6840
Type of machine: Hughes 300c
Ideal loads: multiples of two
Method of carry: racks
Range: Mokihinui, Karamea, Oparara

Coastwide Helicopters Ltd
RD1Rununga
Westland
Ph/fax: 03 731 1823
Mobile: 025 336 792
Type of machine: Hughes 500d

Ideal loads: multiples of four
Method of carry: slingload
Range: Karamea (north) to Wanganui
(south)

Section 7B

Kokatahi Helicopters
RD, Kokatahi
Phone: 03 755 7912
Type of machine: Hughes 300c
Ideal loads: multiples of two
Method of carry: racks
Range: Taipo, Arahura, Kokatahi,
Crooked, Hokitika, Whitcombe,
Whataroa, Perth, Wanganui

Coastwide Helicopters Ltd (see details
Section 7A)

Aspiring Helicopters Ltd
POBox 8, Whataroa
South Westland
Phone: 03 753 4126
a/h 03 753 4118
Type of machine: Hughes 500c
Ideal loads: multiples of four
Method of carry: slingload
Range: Wanganui - Perth - Whataroa

Section 7C

Alpine Adventures
POBox 40, Fox Glacier
Phone: 03 751 0853
Fax: 03 751 0853
Type of machine: Hughes 500 x 2,
Squirrel AS 350b
Ideal loads: multiples of fives or three
Method of carry: slingload
Range: Whataroa, Perth, Wanganui,
Paringa, Landsborough

Haast Heli Adventures
Dave Saxton
POBox 12, Haast
Phone: 03 750 0712
Fax: 03 750 0866
Range: Landsborough, Waiototo,
Waipara

Back Country Helicopters
RD2 Maungawera Rd
Wanaka
Phone: 03 443 1054
Type of machine: Hughes 500d
Ideal loads: multiples of four
Method of carry: slingload
Range: Landsborough, Wilkin, Young,
Waiototo, Waipara

Section 8

Woodbank Helicopters
Box 37, Hanmer Springs
Ph/fax: 03 315 7259
Type of machine: Hughes 300, KH4
Ideal loads: multiples of two
Method of carry: racks or slingload
Range: Upper Waiau

Section 9

Back Country Helicopters (see details
Section 7C)

CLUB LIST

Aoraki Canoe and Kayak Club
31 Queen St
Timaru

Arawa Canoe Club
PO Box 13-177
Christchurch

Army Adventure Club
Waiouru Training Group
Private Bag
Waiouru

Auckland Canoe Club
PO Box 3523
Auckland

Central Otago Whitewater Club
PO Box 214
Alexandra

Hamilton Canoe Club
PO Box 9497
Hamilton

Hauraki Kayak Group
PO Box 46-146
Herne Bay
Auckland

Hawkes Bay Canoe Club
PO Box 883
Napier

Horowhenua Canoe Club
PO Box 268
Levin

Huka Falls Canoe Club
PO Box 972
Taupo

Hutt Valley Canoe Club
PO Box 38-389
Wellington Mail Centre
Wellington

Kaimai Canoe Club
PO Box 2354
Tauranga

Kupe Canoe Club
PO Box 3768
Wellington

Marlborough Canoe Club
PO Box 9
Blenheim

Nelson Canoe Club
PO Box 190
Nelson

New Plymouth Kayak Club
153 Seaview Rd
New Plymouth

Northland Canoe Club
PO Box 755
Whangarei

North Shore Canoe and Youth Club
PO Box 33-492
Takapuna, Auckland

Otago Canoe and Kayak Club
PO Box 5404
Dunedin

Palmerston North Canoe Club
PO Box 1126
Palmerston North

Porirua Canoe and Kayak Club
55 Warspite Ave
Porirua

River City Canoe Club
PO Box 129
Wanganui

Rotorua Canoe Club
PO Box 1458
Rotorua

Ruahine Whitewater Club
71 Salisbury St
Ashhurst

Southland Canoe Club
PO Box 1379
Invercargill

South Taranaki Canoe Club
Inaha Rd RD 11
Hawera

Tawhitikuri Canoe and Kayak Club
OPC
Private Bag
Turangi

University of Canterbury Canoe Club
University Students Association
Private Bag 4800
Christchurch

Victoria University Canoe Club
PO Box 600
Wellington

Waimanui Kayak Club
5 Howard St
Christchurch

Wairarapa Canoe Club
PO Box 630
Masterton

Waitara Kayak Club
Everett Rd RD 8
Inglewood

Waitemata Canoe and Multisports
Club
PO Box 83-037, Edmonton
Waitakere City
Auckland

Westland Canoe Club
PO Box 136
Westport

Whitewater Canoe Club
PO Box 4476
Christchurch

RUNS BY CLASS

These runs are listed at average flows
and may in fact be graded higher or
lower depending on river conditions.

Class II-III

Baton
Buller: Upper
Buller: Howard to Harleys Rock
Buller: Doctor's Creek
Clarence
Grebe
Grey
Hurunui
Karangahake Gorge

Mangles
Mararoa
Maruia
Matakitaki: middle
Matakitaki: earthquake
Mohaka: upper
Motueka: Blue Gums
Opihi
Rangitaiki: lower
Shotover: upper
Waiau: lower
Waikato: Ngaawapurua
Waioeka
Wairau
Waitara
Wakamarina

Class III-IV

Ashley
Buller: Granity
Buller: O'Sullivans to Ariki
Buller: Earthquake
Glenroy
Hokitika: Kakariki Canyon
Hollyford: Gunns Camp
Hollyford: Falls Creek to Marian Bridge
Hutt
Kaituna: Okere Falls
Karamea
Kawarau: Dog Leg
Kawarau: Roaring Meg
Landsborough
Mangahao
Manganui a te ao
Matiri
Mohaka: Te Hoe to Willow Flat
Mokau
Mokihinui
Motu
Ngaruroro
Okuku
Otaki
Rangitaiki: Jeffs Joy
Taieri
Toaroha
Tongariro: Access 10
Tongariro: Access 13
Tongariro: Access 14
Waiau: upper

Waiho
Waihohonu
Waiohine
Waiatoto
Waipori
Wairoa (Nelson)
Waiwhakaiho
Whakapapanui

Class IV-V

Arahura
Arthur
Crooked
Fox
Hollyford: Marian Ck to Gunns Camp
Hooker
Kakapotahi
Kawarau: Citroen
Mangorewa
Manuherikia
Rangitata Gorge
Rangitikei
Routeburn
Shotover Gorge
Taipo
Waikato: Huka Falls
Waipara
Wairoa (Bay of Plenty)
Wanganui
Whakapapa
Whakapapaiti
Whataroa (also has class III put in)
Whitcombe
Wilkin
Young

Class V+ to VI

Burke
Cleddau (also has class IV put in)
Hollyford: Monkey Creek
Kawarau: Nevis Bluff
Kokatahi
Nevis
Oparara
Perth
Turnbull
Tutoko

BIBLIOGRAPHY

Amarel, Grant, *Idaho, the Whitewater State*, Watershed Books, 1990.

Banks and Echardt, *Colorado Rivers and Creeks*, Moenkopi Digital Formations, 1995.

Brailsford, Barry, *Greenstone Trails—The Maori search for pounamu*, A.H. & A.W. Reed Ltd, 1984.

Cobb, John, *Fiordland. The Story of New Zealand's First World Heritage Park*, Cobb/Horwood Publications, 1987.

Cowan, James, and Pomare, Hon. Sir Maui, *Legends of the Maori* , Southern Reprints, Auckland, New Zealand.

Cumberland, Kenneth, and Matthews, Graeme, *Rivers and Lakes in New Zealand*, Whitcoulls, Christchurch, 1985.

Eggar, Graham, *North Island Rivers, A Guide for Canoeists and Rafters*, David Bateman, 1989.

Eggar, Graham, *New Zealand's South Island Rivers*, Nikau Press, 1995.

Jefferies, Margaret, *Adventuring in New Zealand*, Sierra Club, San Francisco, 1993.

Miles, Sue, and Moon, Geoff, *The River—the story of the Waikato*, Heinemann Publishers, 1984.

Pascoe, John, *Exploration New Zealand*, A.H. & A.W. Reed Ltd, 1971.

Reeves, William Pember, *The Long White Cloud*, First published 1898. This edition, Viking Penguin Books, 1987.

Stanley and Holbek, *A guide to the best whitewater in the state of California*, Friends of the River Books, 2nd edition, 1988.

Temple, Philip, *New Zealand Explorers, Great Journeys of Discovery*, Whitcoulls, Christchurch, 1985.

Thornton, Jocelyn, *Field Guide to New Zealand Geology*, Reed Books. First published 1985. This edition 1993.

Wild New Zealand, Readers Digest, Sydney, 1981.

Young, David, and Foster, Bruce, *Faces of the River*, TVNZ Publishing, 1986.